SOUND OF SILENCE

*A festschrift
in honour of
Bishop Dhirendra Kumar Sahu
at his
Shashti-Purti*

SOUND OF SILENCE

*A festschrift
in honour of*
***Bishop Dhirendra Kumar Sahu
at his
Shashti-Purti***

EDITORS

Ravi Tiwari
Bibhudutta Sahu

Tercentenary Publication
2010

Sound of Silence: A festchrift in honour of Bishop Dhirendra Kumar Sahu at His Shashti-Purti – published by the Rev. Dr. Ashish Amos of the Indian Society for Promoting Christian Knowledge (ISPCK), Post Box 1585, 1654, Madarsa Road, Kashmere Gate, Delhi-110006.

© ISPCK, 2010

ISBN : 978-81-8465-090-7

Laser typeset by **ISPCK,** Post Box 1585, 1654, Madarsa Road, Kashmere Gate, Delhi-110006.

Tel: 23866323/22,
e-mail–ashish@ispck.org.in   •   ella@ispck.org.in
website-www.ispck.org.in

Contents

Foreword

It was at the beginning of this year that some of the friends of Bishop D. K Sahu started thinking of celebrating with him the 60th anniversary in life. One of the natural things that one normally associates with this kind of celebration is now a form of collection of articles by the friends involved in theological teaching and pastoral vocation who in most cases are associated with the person concerned in teaching and preaching. With Bishop Sahu this is partially true as he was involved in the other aspects of Christian involvement in service and action. This volume of festschrift is the sincere tribute to the many facets of ministry of Bishop Sahu. The contributors are personal friends, colleagues and relatives of Bishop Sahu and their reflections are interpretive, experiential and personal.

In spite of our request to Bishop Sahu to write short biographical reflections, he in his own humble and gentle ways declined our request. I, as a friend, and Bibhu, as a son have taken on the task of providing a very brief resume of Bishop Sahu.

I have known Dhirendra Kumar Sahu for the past 33 years, which is the entirety of my life. First and foremost, he is my Father. All other designations, titles and recognitions have added to the profile of O'Pa and gained him recognition in the eyes of the world. But as his son, all this was shorn off him as he was our father in the flesh and blood and he would have it no other way. There are only two people who have the privilege of calling him O'Pa / Dad. A lot of my childhood is a little hazy right now but I do recall two endearing images that serve as instant recall. One of them is a photo of my dad hugging, affectionately, the living daylights out of me. It has been one form of affection that rekindles the human bond and reassures me that O'Pa is always just a hug away. It is something that I have carried forward and ensure that my kids never feel the lack of affection and hugs. And the other thing that I did notice about him was his silence. He never forced us into any stream or life choices. And yet in his silence, I learnt to be silent, ponder over the consequences, listen to my inner voice and make a choice. He cared deeply for those around him and went out of his ways to ensure they had a smoother life even though he knew he was going to get hurt in return. His administrative skills, the effortless ease with which he tackled life's problems, the way he took the knocks but refused to lie down and always came out of all the hurdles put in his way with his dignity intact.

I doubt if he could have achieved all this and yet more if he did not have the support of my mom. They say that behind every successful man, there is a woman. Well, in this case, she was never behind him because she was right beside him. She was the balancing factor in his life and nurtured a family of four so that he could continue pursuing his dreams. She bore the heat and dust of the roads just so that the family house could rise from the red ground proving that the foundation was established by her.

To say that I am overwhelmed at this opportunity to pay tribute to my father through this Festschrift would be an understatement. This is a tribute to the Man who has taught me that life will throw up many challenges but if you truly know yourself and trust God, you will be ready to face any challenge. *"The effect of righteousness will be peace and the result of righteousness, quietness and trust forever"* Isaiah 32:17.

Editors

Preface

The common mission of continuing search for truth is an ongoing process. It goes without saying in human and natural sciences. The mission requires developing proposition and rejecting proposition but there is always the joy of innovative insights in making a little contribution in the learning process. In twenty–first century we experience the basic demands of human needs for **friendship and hospitality**. It appears that there tends to be a void that generally does not meet emotional and social needs of the majority. Therefore people do search for **'instant- do-it- yourself' spirituality** that could meet the immediate needs. There is a world out there crying out for hospitality; a world torn apart by discrimination and marginalization, a world broken by wars, terrorism, oppression, prejudice and injustice; a world destroyed by floods, tsunami, hurricane and earthquakes. Therefore there is need to search for a new grammar of discourses for 'friendship **and hospitality'**.

The basic inspiration in doing so is derived from our faith affirmation. The incarnation is all about a **story of home coming of God in silent mode** to the world. *'For God so loved the world that He gave his only son, that whoever believes in him should not perish but have eternal life. For God did not send his son in to the world to condemn the world but in order that the world might be saved through him'*. In the same token the words of Jesus reminds that "Greater love has no one than this that he lay down his life for his friends. **You are my friends if you do what I command.**"(John15:13). The reality of home coming found expression when Mary gave birth to her first-born son and wrapped him in swaddling cloths, and laid him in a manger, because there was no place for them in the Inn. Most interestingly it was neither an exciting moment of noise pollution nor a great celebration but a silent homecoming that has thrilled the generations after generation. The character of such a God is succinctly put by Koshuke Koyama by saying that **God walks only at three miles of an hour**. Following such a God who walks only three miles an hour is overpowering.

A Story is told about a young officer of the regiment under training in 1965. They were rushed to the field but on their way they were feted by the patriotic people encouraging them to put up a good fight. On the way the young officer was told that one of his best friends, a Lieutenant had been killed in action two days back. All the young officers of the regiment were shuddering with fear at their first exposure to high density shelling. Fortunately the regiment was commanded by a Lieutenant Colonel with a formidable reputation for bravery. He gave them a pep talk on how to be courageous.

First of all he consoled them by saying that everybody was scared including himself. That encouraged all of them. If that great man was scared why should they not be? And then he continued. And the catch phrase from the horse's mouth which the young Regiment Officer never forgot after all these years: "Everybody is afraid. But the courageous person is one who is not afraid to be afraid". Shattered as they were, it took some time to register this definition of a courageous person.

Elijah was an energetic and courageous prophet of God that emerges outstandingly in chapter eighteen of the first book of Kings. But the character changes appallingly in chapter nineteen of the same book. The character in eighteen is vocal and over confident but in nineteen the same person is a coward being afraid, ran for his life. He reached a saturation point in his life "I have had enough, Lord," he said. "Take my life". But at that point the encounter takes place that is not only edifying but educative. The Lord said to Elijah, "Go out and stand on the mount before the Lord." And behold, the Lord passed by, and a great and strong wind tore the mountains and broke in pieces the rocks before the Lord, but the Lord was not in the wind. After the wind there was an earthquake, but the Lord was not in the earthquake. And after the earthquake a fire, but the Lord was not in the fire. And after the fire the **sound of low whisper**. And when Elijah heard it, 'he wrapped his face in his cloak and went out and stood at the entrance of the cave. And behold, 'there came a voice to him and said, **"What are you doing here, Elijah?** This narrative of low whisper is preceded by an interesting **occurrence of hospitality of God** by providing "cake of bread baked over hot coals and a jar of water'. This hospitality is before challenging and commissioning Elijah to discharge a responsibility. The Psalmist narrates the hospitality of God by saying "You prepare a Table before me in the presence of my enemies"(Psalm23:5)

Christian vocation requires more than ever before a common basis of spirituality in order to be faithful in mission of God. Christian theology has a challenging task of offering fascinating grammar of discourse that **truth comes as a 'sound of silence'**. It transcends the differences of historical and cultural contexts of eastern and western Christianity. This theological truth is the fountain of spiritual strength challenging the dominance of materialism, consumerism and secularism of our epoch.

Christian theology has a pleasant task of offering genuine **friendship of Christ** in a fragmented and self-centred world. There is a driving force at the heart of the story of the Good Samaritan that Jesus told. Accepting a stranger as a neighbour means opening our hearts to a person we encounter. This is a great leap of faith which removes fear, suspicions and prejudices. This creates opportunity for a healthy relationship. One way of looking at this is to think of **'hospitality'** as grace-driven. It is to place God at the centre of this overgenerous compassion as we get closer to God we get closer to each other. It is God's grace and love that brings neighbourliness in us.

The life that is sought after in our busy culture is in fast forward mode. The people tend to move fast all the time- getting in and getting out, pushing and pulling each other elbowing others to move on. Most sought is a life of convenience and luxury. Today's world is a world of buzz words, sound bites, instant opinions, and packaged discussions and not the least in ecumenical circle the **rainfall of air-conditioned statements** after multiple consultations in air-conditioned rooms. Timothy Gorringe, in his book *'Redeeming Time'* tells, "**To do theology in India is not to do theology at 120° F', as it has been romantically described, but to take part in a struggle between death and life**" (Deut.30:19). Often our discourse does not take cognizance of million but micro stories of faithful and simple people of God who leave footprints in time. A story is well known in Orissa about the father of Bishop Sahu as the **'Barefoot Pastor'.** The ministry of his was for thirty four years in selfless service in remote villages of Orissa. He walked with God and the simple life style, firm commitment, sense of humility and hospitable home was not only an inspiration but exemplary. Such similar people of God around the world not only shape the character formation but set the agenda of ministerial formation. It is these micro stories that have the need of retelling from generation to generation so as not to lose the prospect of truth.

The festschrift on the occasion of the *SHASTI-PURTI* of Bishop D. K. Sahu is an attempt to interlace the ever emerging issues of our time with the overriding paradigm of the **'friendship and hospitality' with the underlying thread of spirituality** by listening to **'the Sound of Silence'.** The contributors are the friends and colleagues of Bishop D. K. Sahu from wide range of theological disciplines and walks of life. Each one has related to the main theme of **'the sound of silence',** which is a sign through their hospitality of love and friendship.

Late Rev Birendra Kumar Sahu & Mrs. Pramodini Sahu

Bishop Dhirendra Kumar Sahu & Mrs Manjusree Sahu

Bishop Sahu with his 2 sons, daughters-in-law and 2 granddaughters

Bishop Sahu with 3 generations of the Sahu family

Chapter - 1

Theological Creativity Today: Worship and Conversation

David F. Ford

It was Christmas Day in a town among tea plantations in the Diocese of the East Himalayas. About a thousand people had gathered for the consecration of their first church building, after years of worshipping in small groups scattered over a wide area. Even though the building was not yet finished the congregation had been determined that it should be consecrated by their Bishop, Dhirendra Sahu, before he left to work with the National Council of Churches in India the next month. In the course of many hours of worship, speeches, feasting, storytelling and conversation I learned a good deal about his remarkable ministry there, partly from the many unsolicited expressions of appreciation and respect, but also by simply observing his quiet, warm presence among the people.

That visit to India by myself, my wife and three children was a rich experience for all of us, make possible by Dhirendra's and Manju's generous hospitality, strategic planning and thoughtful advice. For me it was also the fulfilment of a desire that had been kindled many years earlier by Dhirendra himself. I had supervised his doctoral dissertation on the origins and theology of the Church of North India and, as so often happens, I felt I had learned more through the process from my student than he had from me. Dhirendra's careful study of the original documents of the negotiations leading to CNI's formation, combined with perceptive and constructive thinking about the appropriate theology for it, as well as the ways he and Manju talked about their church and country, made me long to visit that part of India. In the years that followed, I was able to visit South India more than once, and had got to know several clergy and other members of CNI, but it was only as Dhirendra was about to leave his diocese that the opportunity came to visit it. Not the least important part of the visit were intensive conversations, in the context of wonderful hospitality, with North Indian Christians and many others. What happened to the picture of CNI I had formed through Dhirendra's doctoral study many years previously? There were many points of contact, but overall the reality of the church on the ground and through the eyes of some leaders and non-members made me realise yet again how necessary it is to have first-hand involvement. The experience of that congregation among the tea plantations did not fit any previous picture, and each meeting and conversation reinforced the obvious truth: face to face relationships, witnessing the body of Christ in person, and the sharing of testimony together – these give access to the reality of a church in ways that books, history, and theology (and I would add the media too) cannot.

Yet here there is a danger. It is fatally easy to emphasise 'experience' and the reality of the local, grassroots church in contrast to what is in books and other media. But as soon as you look at what goes into the making of the experience of the local Christian community in North India or North London you realise that there can be no romantic picture of a reality somehow separate from the complexities of history and theology. Every such community has been shaped by a particular history and continues to see itself in relation to its past – the vital question is how true and discerning its picture of that past is. Each community has to face questions that make theological judgements unavoidable: What sense can be made of suffering and death? What should we teach our children? How do we relate to those of other faiths and none? How should we respond to injustice? What about scientific understandings of the world? What about political commitment, abortion, violence, war, money, corruption, sex, family life, business ethics? What about baptism or Lord's Supper/Holy Communion/Eucharist/Mass? Should we have bishops, elders, or democratic consensus on everything? How should the Bible be interpreted in relation to these questions and many, many more?

Theology as Creative Wisdom

If I were summing up the core issue here I would name it as 'wisdom'. In relation to each of those questions there are wiser and more foolish answers for a particular community, but it is rarely easy to decide which is which. And it is clear that no one individual has a monopoly on the wisdom needed to answer such questions. The wisdom must be worked out together, above all in conversation, but also by drawing on the wisdom and understanding of the past, of people in other parts of the world, and of those who can only contribute through books and other media.

But wisdom has for many people a flavour of what is ancient, rather conservative, and more for the old than the young. That is not actually true of biblical wisdom, which is 'hot', acutely relevant to the young, and often very adventurous. While spending over a decade writing a book on wisdom, I was more and more impressed by the daring wisdom of the book of Job, which became central to two chapters and helped shape the whole book.[1] Job is seen as very wise at the beginning of the story, but even wiser by the end. He

---

[1] David F. Ford, *Christian Wisdom. Desiring God and Learning in Love* (Cambridge University Press, Cambridge 2010).

has responded to terrible, bewildering suffering by passionately asking questions and seeking a wisdom that both honours God and genuinely engages with his situation. His friends offer packages of received wisdom; Job knows that wisdom but knows also that the past formulae cannot cope with what is happening to him. So he cries out, argues, searches, experiments intellectually and imaginatively, and refuses to be satisfied with anything less than deep, fresh engagement with God. The result is not a neat theology, but a wisdom-seeking that has inspired generation after generation, especially when faced with new situations and great suffering.

My conclusion is that the most adequate short description of theology is as God-related wisdom. At its best it takes seriously the call of God and the cries of humanity, and is concerned not only for knowledge and understanding but also for imaginative richness, discerning judgements, and how to cope with often intractable, insoluble problems. It is a wisdom that especially recognises that God invites us into a future that demands fresh thinking and creative responses beyond what the past has provided.

Elements of Theological Creativity

What are the elements of such wise theological creativity? Reflecting on more than twenty years working as editor for three editions of *The Modern Theologians*,[2] which tries to cover Christian theology around the world since 1918, I recently realised that I had never asked that question directly. I have since been working on it,[3] and came up with four interconnected elements that seem to me to be the essentials in forming the 'ecology' for good theology:

---

[2] David F. Ford with Rachel Muers (Eds) *The Modern Theologians. An Introduction to Christian Theology since 1918* Third Edition (Blackwell, Oxford 2005).

[3] For a longer account of what follows in this paper see the forthcoming *The Future of Christian Theology* (Wiley Blackwell, Oxford 2010).

- *Wise and creative retrieval of the past.* This is about interpreting the Bible above all, but also traditions and histories, and the life and thought of significant people, movements, groups and institutions. Christian theology must deal with the past, discerning how best to relate to it so as to resource the present and the future.

- *Wise and creative engagement in the present with God, church and world.* The first, incomparable engagement is with God. This pervades all other engagements and is above all 'for God's sake' – the great commandment is to love God with all one's heart, mind, soul and strength. The second is with the church: to be Christian is to be part of the body of Christ, the people of God, so Christian theology must in some sense be church theology. The third is with the world God has created and loves.

- *Wise and creative thinking.* This is partly about basic intellectual good practice, such as asking appropriate questions, thinking logically and honestly, using experience and evidence appropriately, ordering arguments clearly, seeking and testing insights, and learning who are the models of good practice to whom appeal can be made. It is also about the more creative side of thinking, its imaginative and inventive aspect that conceives new insights and possibilities, often improvising on past positions in relation to new understanding or contexts.

- *Wise and creative expression and communication.* Good theology can become better theology through being better expressed. Form and content are closely related and many appropriate genres, styles, arts and media are needed for theology to find its right match of form and content for particular groups. Since theologians often have limited gifts in these areas, this calls for writers, artists, composers, song-writers, programme-makers, film-makers and others.

One twentieth century theologian whose work unites all of these is Dietrich Bonhoeffer. His theology is rooted in the Bible, the early church, the Reformation and modernity. Throughout his adult life till his execution by the Nazis in 1945 at the age of 39 he was passionately engaged in many spheres of life, including the local church in working class Berlin, the international ecumenical movement, the Confessing Church that opposed the German Christians who supported the Nazis (his book on community life that emerged from this shows his understanding and practice of involvement with God in prayer), and the secular resistance to Hitler. His works are full of fresh, creative thinking, both critical and constructive. And he was a remarkably effective communicator through many genres – academic monographs, popular books, sermons, letters, papers, lectures, poems and fiction. In all of this he was richly collegial, and it is that aspect of theological creativity that I want to concentrate on in the rest of this paper.

Collegial Creativity Focused through Worship

Christian theology is never just an individual matter. It is inextricable from relating to other people and to God. Above all, as it engages with the past and present for the sake of God's future, its creativity depends upon many types of belonging. How adequate can the labour of retrieval and description be if it is done by only one scholar? What sense does a lone individual's theological engagement with contemporary life make? Some popular ideas of creative thinking imagine it being done by an isolated genius, but experience suggests the opposite: the best thinkers are usually those who are most deeply engaged with the thought of others, alive and dead, and who have the best teachers and conversation partners. It is perhaps in creative expression that the utter sociability of theology is clearest: the very words and forms used are learnt from others and shared with others; the receiving of tradition is the condition for improvising on it, and any innovation must persuade others of its authenticity if it is not to be seen as just odd or idiosyncratic rather than creative. So a fundamental, repeated question for any theologian is: where, and with whom, do I belong?

In theological terms, 'creativity' (understood analogously as part of what it means to be created in the image of one's Creator) might be seen as what serves to open people to God and God's future – 'the Kingdom of God'. This is at heart a matter of being loved and loving. It should not be sentimentalised: God's love is satisfied with nothing less than all God has created us to be. The 'all' includes body, intellect, heart, imagination and will, energised and inspired by God's Spirit to love God and all God has created and loves. The ultimate invitation is to a face-to-face joy that is spoilt by anything less than wholehearted, understanding love. Given the sort of world we inhabit, with many deep-set resistances to loving and being loved that are embedded in ourselves, others and whole groups, cultures, institutions and societies, we desperately need a wisdom of love and we also desperately need other people to share in the drama of loving. Theology is part of that drama, and its goal is to think together the love of God's wisdom and the wisdom of God's love. The way to that goal is through a world that constantly distracts, dispirits and even traumatises those committed to wise loving. But it is a way that can hardly be travelled at all without companions in understanding and loving.

The fundamental forms of belonging come together on this path: belonging to God and to each other as fellow-Christians and as fellow-human beings. This is a threefold dynamic, in which each can deepen and intensify the other.

A helpful key concept is that of covenant. The identity of the Christian theologian is covenantal in a strong sense – I think of the annual Methodist Covenant Service which expresses this with remarkable power. Belonging to God with other people means that all thinking is within that relationship, trying to be as alert as possible to its significance for all areas of understanding and living.

This above all involves thinking immersed in prayer and worship, enacting a fundamental orientation towards God and other people, springing from thankful appreciation of the covenant love of God. Like marriage, it is a state, a commitment, and a way of life that thrives on mutual communication in joy, truth and love, but that can also plunge into agony of mind and heart. Worship is a particularly good sign of the shared nature of theology. It performs the identity of a church before God, and it embodies in communal form all four elements of theological creativity.

So, worship is about shared retrieval, resourced by the past of scripture and tradition. Even when it is not directly quoting scripture it is often indebted to it, and its language and structure embody the outcomes of centuries of communal experience, debate and discernment. Without that, for example, the prominence in many liturgies of Trinitarian statements, such as 'Glory be to the Father and to the Son and to the Holy Spirit', is unthinkable. The choice of scriptural passages in lectionaries helps form the mind and imagination of a community year after year. A basic pattern of retrieval is embodied in a church's calendar. By taking part in a liturgy one is sharing in the community's central form of retrieval.

Worship is also a present joint engagement, above all with God. Cries of address and praise, exclamations spoken or sung, and bodily movements - these acknowledge the central, encompassing, shared reality of the presence of God. There is also engagement with church and world. Preaching and teaching are where scripture and tradition are thought through in relation to the present and future. The contents of thanksgivings, intercessions and petitions are indicators of a community's concerns and involvements in the world.

Worship also encodes seminal, creative theological thinking of the past in its uses of scripture, in creeds that distil classic teachings, in the shape of liturgies, and in hymns and songs. It allows, too, for new thinking in sermons, prayers and improvisations on habitual forms. *Lex orandi, lex credendi* (the rule for praying is the rule for believing) has long been a commonplace of Christian thought, though not uncontroversial. Its wisdom is in recognising the deep mutuality of prayer and faith, together with their sociality (taking *lex* as something recognised by a whole community); and thought is intrinsic to both of them.

The twentieth century was perhaps the most creative in the history of Christian worship. There was an explosion of new music, songs, hymns, chants, ritual and dance, and revivals of many traditional forms. The Roman Catholic Church radically revised its liturgies and began celebrating them in scores of the world's languages. The liturgies and lectionaries of many other churches were revised, often allowing for wide local variations. It is no accident that the twentieth century was also so creative in theology. Every liturgical development has required theological thinking and discernment, and a vast amount of intellectual and imaginative energy has gone into these transformations of worship. There are also the daily and weekly theological demands on those who organise and lead worship, trying in lively and relevant ways to shape congregational services, baptisms, confirmations, ordinations, weddings, funerals, feast days and events such as the Methodist Covenant Service. Add to all this the thinking that is stimulated in ordinary worshippers as they pray, sing, listen, discuss and respond variously to worship (for example, by relating it to the rest of their lives), and it becomes clear that this might be seen as the sphere of maximal and most explicit Christian theological creativity.

Then there is creative expression and communication. The inseparability of creative thought from creative expression is especially important for worship, which offers forms of word and action to hundreds of millions of people week after week. It is not just that every word counts; each genre, juxtaposition, ordering, gesture, article of clothing, musical accompaniment, architectural environment and cultural setting is also part of the performance and its meaning.

Overall, therefore, worship is something like the genetic code of a Christian community. It condenses core meanings that are transmitted across the generations, and it allows for variations. Theological thinking both helps to shape it and is shaped by it. A fundamental discernment to be made about any theology is whether it rings true with the worship of one or more churches. In other words, does it share the 'genetic code' or 'grammar of faith' to be found in worship? Deciding this, of course, itself requires theological discussion, and there are times when a community decides to innovate. But few things illustrate the joint, shared character of Christian theology more than the social processes through which worship is shaped.

The lesson from this for theology (whether ordinary or more academic theological thinking) is both that thought needs to be shaped through long term, faithful immersion in worship with fellow-Christians and also that there is a responsibility to join with others in serving the theological health of worship, including wise innovation. Worship is where the code is transmitted, the grammar learnt. It is the performance that, when done well, condenses and communicates formative retrieval, engagement with God, church and world, thought and expression. To internalise a rich practice of worship is to expand the capacity for fresh creativity. Those who write classics are usually those who are steeped in that language's classics. Like a jazz player whose mastery of instrument and repertoire enables virtuoso improvisations on well-known themes, the theologian who is steeped in worship is more likely to offer discernments and proposals that not only ring true with past and present Christian wisdom but also creatively add to its sum.

Collegial Creativity through Conversation

Yet worship is still only one of the dimensions of the church with which theology is concerned. The two other principal ones are community life, with its catechesis and education, pastoral care, social activities, organisations and institutional structures; and mission beyond the Christian community, in evangelism and various forms of dialogue and service to the common good. These go on locally, regionally, nationally and internationally. Theological thinking needs to happen in each aspect and at each level, and also to think about them together. It is clear that the seeking of wisdom in all these areas has to be conversational and collaborative if it is to be true and fruitful. This is by no means to deny the importance of individual formation and responsibility, but to stress the primacy of belonging.

One conception of the church that emerges from this discussion is as a school of creative wisdom. The wisdom of God and God's purposes is to be learnt with others through worship, community living and discerning engagement in many spheres of life, and the worship-centred church is a school for that. Yet it is not the only place where wisdom is sought and where learning and teaching go on. There are other complementary forms of belonging, some Christian and some mixed with those of other faiths or none, through which theological wisdom can be pursued. These include forms of collegiality that are centred on learning and teaching theology in a more educational, academic sense. If one were to ask where a church seeks scholarly and theological wisdom as it goes about deciding its forms of worship, the answer is usually: from those teaching in academic institutions. 'Collegiality' is a term for the jointness of those places, where theology is taught by a group of colleagues.

If one imagines Christian theological education around the world today as an ecosystem, by far the largest niche is made up of church institutions of many sorts. These range from courses set up by local or regional church bodies, through study groups, Bible colleges, religious orders, distance learning organisations and seminaries, to research centres and Christian universities. These are the places where most of the Christians who have the chance to learn any theology do so, and also where most of the vast company of clergy, preachers, teachers, catechists, evangelists, youth leaders, religious broadcasters, writers and interested lay people are educated.

There is also another, smaller niche (such as the University of Cambridge where I work), where Christian theology is done in settings that are not solely Christian. I see such mixed settings as a healthy development that is not necessarily in tension or competition with the larger niche. On the contrary, both niches contribute to the flourishing of the whole ecology. Theology learnt and taught in places where there are teachers and students who belong to different religious and non-religious or secular traditions can be of great value in societies that are complexly religious and secular. In society at large different forms of belonging must try to work out how to get along together; it is therefore deeply appropriate that there be places of education, scholarship and research where it is possible for those with diverse commitments to tackle the many questions concerning these commitments, including those raised by the religions, between the religions and about the religions (and not least the questions raised by those who do not belong to them).

In addition to institutional settings there are also many other settings where theology is done. Just think of the networks, movements and innumerable other possible places where theological questions are raised. One thing in common across all of these and the institutional settings, both Christian and mixed, is the importance of conversation.

Conversation is a marvellously (yet somewhat annoyingly) flexible term, ranging from the most casual encounter to a lifetime of intense interaction. Theological creativity requires all levels. I will conclude this paper with some reflections first on the middle range of conversations, and then on some of the most intensive.

The Middle Range of Conversations

Most theological conversations that are more than casual happen within structured environments. In the academic study of theology beyond one's home institution this means conferences, activities of societies for the study of aspects of theology, and increasing numbers of training days, seminars, broadcasts, media events, dialogues and discussions after lectures. Surrounding all these is a penumbra of informal encounters, emails, telephone conversations, chat rooms, blogs, twittering, and occasionally letters.

Essential for the organised events are the organisers, whose theological role is often ignored. Organisational creativity is as precious as other sorts, and requires all four of the elements of retrieval, engagement, imaginative thought and expression. Good organisers write their theology in fruitful interactions between people. They choose themes and people, shape sequences and schedules, attend to the practical aspects of travel, food, accommodation and financing, liaise diplomatically, cope with crises, and have a maestro conductor's sense of timing. Unwise judgements and decisions make the event impoverished or even counter-productive. Wise organisation is one condition for the possibility of the wonderful conversations, formal and informal, that can happen.

The future health of Christian theology partly depends, therefore, on the discernment and dedication of creative organisers who shape the agendas and environments needed for high quality face to face communication. It is important for the established long term conversations to continue; it is also vital to discern which recent ones to concentrate on and which new ones to initiate. In Randall Collins' massive sociological study of intellectual creativity in philosophy over millennia in many cultures (including Greece, India, China, Japan, the Roman Empire and global modernity), the simple central conclusion is that a critical condition for the best philosophy is intensive conversation. The most influential philosophies have been generated in face to face conversation between contemporaries and across generations, and have been sustained and developed by institutions that provided the necessary conditions.[4]

---

[4] Randall Collins, *The Sociology of Philosophies: A Global Theory of Intellectual Change* (Harvard University Press, Cambridge MA 1998).

The same is undoubtedly true for theology. The lesson is simple: engage in conversation, encourage it, and nurture the settings where it can flourish.

Intensive Conversation: Commitment, Apprenticeship and Friendship

With whom do we live, collaborate closely and try to realise God's future for others and ourselves? Conversation is more important than ever in these relationships where communication is complemented by commitment. Some of the most formative theology is stimulated through relationships of cohabitation – meaning not just family life but certain localities and communities, religious orders, retreat centres, and other places where people live together with some degree of common intention.

In these contexts of living and working it becomes clearer why it makes sense for theology to be conceived as wisdom. Theological thinking here tries to make deep and practical connections with Christian faith and experience, and to discern with others, who may not share one's faith, how to shape life and work. This thinking is often, of course, not labelled 'theological', but yet is directly related to the purposes of God in the world. It is perhaps the most pervasive sort of theology, fed by whatever has been learnt through being part of a worshipping community and in other ways. One of the key tasks of theology in educational and academic settings is to inspire and nourish such everyday thinking. This might be seen as part of a broader aim, in conversation and collaboration with those of other faiths and none, to shift our 'knowledge society' into a 'wisdom society'.

In addition to such ordinary settings there are also more specialised contexts for intensive conversations, such as religious movements, theological 'schools' or movements, and activist groups that campaign on a specific issue. But I want to conclude with two that are most relevant to this Festschrift.

The first is apprenticeship in academic theology, the final stage of which is working on a doctoral dissertation. When I think of those years working with Dhirendra on his doctorate what I remember most is hours of conversation around his fascinating work, drawing on thinking that was in its turn indebted to hours of conversation with my own teachers and mentors over many years. Such conversations, in many ways as formative for the teacher as for the student, are at the heart of whatever wisdom and creativity one might be able to achieve in our field.

The second is friendship. A founder member of the ecumenical movement once summed up to me what he thought was one of the main secrets of whatever it had achieved: friendships. He named some deep one-to-one friendships, often initiated and sustained with considerable courage, that were at the heart of the strong bonding, creative thinking, practical initiatives and seminal statements that went into the ecumenical movement. My study and experience confirm this. In the ecosystem of Christian theology today I have often found that the most lively creative wisdom is rooted in the intensive conversation of long term friendships. Those of us who know Dhirendra and Manju as friends have been privileged to have a glimpse of the quality of wisdom that continues to sustain one of the most remarkable ecumenical ventures in Christian history, the Church of North India. May they continue to be a blessing to the church, their friends and each other!

Chapter - 2

Free Churchman, Bishop, Missionary Ecumenist

Nicholas J. Wood

It is both a privilege and a pleasure to offer these reflections in recognition of the significant contribution to the life of the universal church by one whom it is a delight to know as a friend as well as a colleague. We first encountered one another as graduate students in Oxford a quarter of a century ago and we have kept in touch ever since. We have met again in Oxford from time to time, but also at Serampore College where he served with great distinction, and I have also enjoyed the hospitality of the Sahu home in Siliguri during his period as Bishop of the Eastern Himalaya. A Baptist who became a bishop, an Oriya who found a place in Oxford as also in West Bengal and the Himalayas, an Indian who is at home as a citizen of the world; all this reflects Bishop Sahu's true ecumenical spirit, one whose horizons have always remained as wide as his roots in Christ have stayed deep. The title of this chapter truly reflects such a man, but the main protagonist for this discussion is not D.K. Sahu but another noted Free Churchman who became a founding bishop in the Church of South India, and developed into perhaps the most significant missionary ecumenist of the 20th century, Bishop Lesslie Newbigin.[1] I hope to show that Newbigin's whole theology is built on an approach to the restoration of relationship between God and humanity which may offer a basis for all true hospitality.

The career of Lesslie Newbigin (1909-1998) is sufficiently well known to require only the briefest of introductions.[2] Brought up in a devout Presbyterian household in Newcastle-upon-Tyne and educated at the Quaker Leighton Park School in Berkshire, Newbigin read Geography at Queen's College, Cambridge, followed by theological education at Westminster College; he was ordained in the Church of Scotland for service as a missionary in India and sailed for the subcontinent in 1936. Except for six years with the International Missionary Council and its successor body in the World Council of Churches based in Geneva, India was to be Newbigin's sphere of service for nearly forty years. He became a founding bishop in the United Church of South India, first in Madurai and later in Madras. Following 'retirement' in 1974 there followed responsibility for teaching mission studies at the Selly Oak College in Birmingham subsequently coupled with an active inner-city pastorate for the United Reformed Church of which he was elected national Moderator for 1978-79.[3]

Throughout this long and busy career in the service of the Church, Bishop Newbigin maintained a steady flow of books and articles concerned with the nature of the Christian message and the

---

[1] Another ecumenical bishop whom it was my privilege to meet; a version of the following discussion appears in Nicholas J. Wood, *Faiths and Faithfulness: Pluralism, Mission and Dialogue in the thought of Kenneth Cragg and Lesslie Newbigin*, (Paternoster Press, Milton Keynes 2009).

[2] See the useful biographical sketch in Paul Weston *Lesslie Newbigin Missionary Theologian* (SPCK London 2006) pp1-13 and the Introduction: A Man in Christ to Geoffrey Wainwright's very full 'theological biography' *Lesslie Newbigin A Theological Life* (OUP Oxford 2000), pp3-28.

[3] See Bishop Newbigin's own account in his autobiography *Unfinished Agenda* (SPCK London 1985).

life of the Church in the modern world. A recurring theme in the thought of Lesslie Newbigin is the question of the salvation of humanity. As he indicates in one of his earliest studies, *Sin and Salvation*[4] for him a crucial question is how the 'finished work of Christ' is related to the life of the believer and the believing community - "How does salvation become ours?".[5] This was the question which had been posed for him as a theological student in Cambridge, and the answer that he formulated then remained true throughout his life and work. He expressed it in strongly Pauline terms, for it was in wrestling with the Epistle to the Romans that his convictions were formed, "This was a turning point in my theological journey. I began my study as a typical liberal. I ended it with a strong conviction about 'the finished work of Christ', about the centrality and objectivity of the atonement accomplished on Calvary".[6] Although he suggests that this new understanding "made me much more of an evangelical than a liberal",[7] he did not fall into the common evangelical trap of narrow individualism, but rather maintained a corporate and indeed cosmic sense of the work of Christ. It is precisely this awareness of the universality of the Christian proclamation, which poses the difficult question of how this salvation is to be manifested on such a scale. How can 'the finished work of Christ' be complete when so many communities and peoples are in ignorance of it and of the claim of the Church that 'Jesus is Lord'? Here we see something of the strength of the missionary imperative which runs throughout Newbigin's thinking. There is a necessary tension between 'the finished work of Christ' and the 'unfinished agenda' of the Church, a body that Newbigin repeatedly characterizes as "a community *in via*, on its way to the ends of the earth and to the end of time".

---

[4] Written with the needs of village catechists in mind (SCM London, 1956).

[5] Newbigin, *Sin and Salvation*, p8.

[6] Newbigin, *Unfinished Agenda*, p30.

[7] Newbigin, *Unfinished Agenda*, p31.

Newbigin expounds the human situation in terms of humanity's essential self-contradiction: we are at odds with each other, with the natural world, with our inner selves, and with God, which is "the basic contradiction on which all else rests".[8] This fundamental contradiction results in bondage to the hostile forces of the universe. Salvation therefore means release from this bondage and the resolution of these contradictions. It means 'wholeness' and the fulfilling of God's original purposes for humanity and the whole of creation. In his later writings Newbigin suggested that it is the denial of 'purpose' and the attempt to live without it, that is the particular expression of the human predicament for contemporary western humanity, "We all engage in purposeful activity, and we judge ourselves and others in terms of success in achieving the purposes that we set before ourselves. Yet we accept as the final product of this purposeful activity a picture of the world from which purpose has been eliminated".[9]

The modern scientific world-view is a mechanistic one, which can admit of no sense of purpose, yet in the realm of human relationships the whole discussion is dominated by concepts of 'the good' against which differing and contradictory accounts of purpose are assessed.[10] For Newbigin denial of purpose is tantamount to denial of God, and is therefore a contemporary expression of that fundamental disobedience to God traditionally called sin: "the essence of sin is unbelief, and the opposite of sin is faith".[11] Its inevitable result is seen in the human self-contradiction already outlined.

However, humanity is made in the image of God, and although sin causes us to contradict our true nature, it is not totally destroyed.

---

[8] Newbigin, *Sin and Salvation*, p13, cf Wainwright *Theological Life*, pp38ff.

[9] Newbigin, *Foolishness to the Greeks* (SPCK London 1986), p78.

[10] Newbigin, *Foolishness to the Greeks*, p66 & pp78f.

[11] Newbigin, *Sin and Salvation*, p20.

Newbigin likens the image of God in humanity to the reflection of the moon in water, it may be distorted or even totally hidden, it depends on the relationship between the two. Nor can the image be discovered in the individual, but only in relationship, especially in man-and-woman bound together in love. Humanity is made for love, but in failing to acknowledge and love God we are driven in upon ourselves. Sin thus comes to be self-love and idolatry, again expressed not just in the lives of individuals, but also in the lives of communities, of nations and of states. This idolatry is the result of the constant threat and anxiety experienced by the self which places itself at the centre of the universe, and which is expressed in the search for security. Idolatry is at the heart of much religious practice for this too is but an expression of the human search for certainty and security.[12]

The human situation produced by sin is real and terrible; its objectivity and inevitability are well conveyed by the traditional Indian concept of *karma*, although this fails in Newbigin's view to comprehend the corporate nature of sin and the collective guilt of the human race. For Newbigin there is no ultimate explanation for sin, but its reality as a "dark mystery of life"[13] is all too evident. It is impossible for humanity to save itself; for salvation requires a change of will and it is here that sin is at its most pervasive. God's wrath opposes sin and its destructive power and keeps all things in being, but only his mercy and grace bring salvation.[14] It is clear that all this reflects not just the opening chapters of Genesis, but also the Pauline interpretation of the human situation as outlined in the first chapter of Romans. Newbigin is convinced of the truth of John 3:16. God has acted in history for the salvation of the human race; it is God who is the source of salvation, springing from that eternal love which is expressed in the doctrine of the Trinity. As one

---

[12] Newbigin, *Sin and Salvation*, pp26ff.
[13] Newbigin, *Sin and Salvation*, p39.
[14] Newbigin, *Sin and Salvation*, p42.

reviewer puts it: "Newbigin holds to and expounds those theological scandals which alienate other faiths - the Trinity and its expression in the cross, so that mission is seen as faith, hope and love in action."[15]

The doctrines of the Trinity and the Incarnation, the centre and climax of which is the Cross, stand at the heart of Newbigin's understanding of God and the divine action in the world. This influence can be traced in almost everything he writes. Newbigin retains a firm grasp of the link between being and relationship. The corporate element is central to his understanding not only of the human situation, but also to his understanding of the nature of God; relationship is therefore seen as an essential structure of salvation itself: "Interpersonal relatedness belongs to the very being of God. Therefore there can be no salvation for man except in relatedness."[16] Newbigin is equally clear that this salvation is focused in the person and work of Jesus of Nazareth: "Jesus was a man who lived among men in Palestine nineteen centuries ago; but he also spoke and acted as God's own representative with full power to claim the obedience which man owes to God".[17] At the heart of this event stands the cross, although it cannot, and indeed must not, be separated from Jesus' life on the one hand, and his resurrection and ascension on the other. Although Newbigin recognised that no one theory of atonement is adequate, nevertheless the witness of Scripture and Tradition does allow some statements to be made. First that Jesus' death was both necessary and the will of the Father, for: "The holy love of God can only make terms with the sin of men at the cost of suffering and death".[18] Secondly, the death of Jesus arises out of his self-identification with sinners as

---

[15] Cyril Davey, on *The Open Secret*, in *The Expository Times* (Vol. 91, 1979-80) p157.

[16] Newbigin, *The Open Secret* (2nd edition SPCK London 1986), p78.

[17] Newbigin, *Sin and Salvation*, p59.

[18] Newbigin, *Sin and Salvation*, p55.

expressed most profoundly in the 'cry of dereliction' from the cross.[19] Next, that it is a means of life for the world,[20] and a revelation, in fact *the* revelation, of God's love, for "love must be expressed in deeds".[21]

True forgiveness is not about punishment and penalty, but the restoration of relationship. Whilst the metaphor of ransom cannot be pressed too far, "a price had to be paid,"[22] but this should not be seen in terms of propitiation, of which God is never the object in Scripture. Scripture is definite that what God requires is not sacrifice but obedience, and in the obedience unto death of Jesus true sacrifice has been made and therefore: "The death of Jesus thus provides in reality what the sacrifices of the Old Testament provide only in symbol".[23] For those who would question this whole scheme of salvation because of the so-called "scandal of particularity" (that is, how can a single event in time and space be of universal significance?), Newbigin neatly stands the argument on its head. Precisely *because* human beings are creatures of time and space, caught up in the stream of history, salvation must have historical form and expression. Thus:

> "God, according to the Bible, is concerned with the redemption of the whole human race and of the whole created world ... the way of its working involves at every point the recreation of true human relationships and of true relationship between man and the rest of the created order. Its centre is necessarily a deed wrought at an actual point in history and at a particular place."[24]

That this is so depends upon the essential unity of humanity (and for that matter of the universe), for he argues always for the

---

[19] Mark 15:34.

[20] e.g. John 6 & 12:32

[21] Newbigin, *Sin and Salvation*, p71; see also pp62-69 for Newbigin's more detailed commentary on the death of Christ.

[22] Newbigin, *Sin and Salvation*, p82.

[23] Newbigin *Sin and Salvation*, p87.

[24] Newbigin, *The Household of God*, (SCM London 1958) p99.

fundamental unity of the human race, there is only one story, one history. This means that the biblical story is not a separate story; rather it is part of the unbroken fabric of world history. Christians believe that it is in this place that the pattern has been disclosed, even though the weaving is not yet finished. "Christian faith is thus a way of understanding world history which challenges and relativizes all other models by which the meaning of history is interpreted".[25]

Bound up with all of this is Newbigin's reassertion of the doctrine of election, which for George Hunsberger is the clue to Newbigin's whole theology.[26] Election involves the choosing of the one for the blessing of the many, beginning with the call of Abraham and the foundation of the 'Chosen People', through the notion of 'Remnant' (a *saving* remnant rather than one which is merely *saved*), until the final focus is upon the One, the Christ. Then the movement again becomes outward and expansive, from the first witnesses, through the Church to the whole world. The Bible thus compels the Church to say what it would not dare say for itself, "God leads the world to its consummation through the apostolate of the Church".[27] For Newbigin the doctrine of election is not only compatible with the nature of God and the nature of humanity, "it is the *only* principle congruous with the nature of God's redeeming purpose,"[28] that is, redemption as relatedness and in relationships. A particular view of the nature of redemption or salvation is thus fundamental to Newbigin's thought, of which the doctrine of election is but a

---

[25] Newbigin, *Open Secret*, p99.

[26] See his doctoral dissertation *"The Missionary Significance of the Biblical Doctrine of Election as a Foundation for a Theology of Cultural Plurality in the Missiology of J. E. Lesslie Newbigin"*, George R. Hunsberger, Princeton 1987. Subsequently published as *Bearing the Witness of the Spirit: Lesslie Newbigin's Theology of Cultural Plurality* (Eerdmans, Grand Rapids, 1998).

[27] Newbigin, *Household of God*, p139.

[28] Newbigin, *Household of God*, p101.

function. To sum up his whole argument let Newbigin again speak for himself:

> "There is an actual sphere of redemption, of which the historical centre is Jesus Christ incarnate, crucified, risen and ascended. From that centre the word of salvation goes out to all the earth, the nations are baptised, the Lord's table is spread, a real community is built up - all by the living sovereign working of the Holy Spirit. It is here in this visible community, that God is savingly at work reconciling the world to Himself, precisely because the salvation which He purposes is not merely private and spiritual but corporate and cosmic."[29]

It is clear from all of this that human life, both in sin and salvation, is corporate and, in the end, cosmic. Present experience of relationship is a pointer to the consummation of the divine purpose when all things will be caught up into that fully reciprocal relationship which is signified by the doctrine of the Trinity. Such discussion of the most fundamental points of Christian doctrine issues in the call to mission, the call to bear witness, and Newbigin emphasises that in all this the believer speaks "the language of testimony".[30] What is claimed is a relationship with 'Him who has spoken', and if the question is put 'Has He spoken?' the answer can only come in the realm of testimony and witness.

The Christian Church is therefore the community of witness, living in the tension between what Newbigin has characterized as the "perfect and future tenses" based on the 'indicative' of the new reality experienced in Christ.[31] It expresses itself through the relationships of the new community which Christ forms, and in its words and actions. Newbigin is in no doubt about the validity of the Church, nor of its divine commission,[32] again arguing from his understanding of the nature of salvation as relational:

---

[29] Newbigin, *Household of God*, p131.

[30] Newbigin, *Foolishness to the Greeks*, p91.

[31] Newbigin, *A Faith for this One World?* (SCM London 1961) pp84ff.

[32] Newbigin is certain: "There can be no question that Jesus intended to be represented in all the plenitude of his power, by his own chosen and commissioned people." *Household of God*, p62.

> "God's way of salvation is not by enabling a few individuals to grasp the truth - either by mystical union, or by intellectual enquiry, or by being given one universal and inerrant revelation in code or book; it is by calling a people to Himself, that they may be with Him and that He may send them forth."[33]

The Church is thus chosen and called by God in order to be the bearer of blessing to the world. This pattern is congruous with the nature of God, the nature of the human race and the nature of salvation, as Newbigin has outlined it. Therefore the Church has a vital role in the process of salvation of which a "universalist" theology takes no account. For if God can and does bestow his grace indiscriminately, then the Church is no essential part of the whole scheme of salvation, indeed God himself ignores it.[34] Newbigin argues that such a position is intolerable, not only in that it fails to do justice either to the nature of the Church or the nature of salvation, but because it also violates the fundamental freedom which God has granted to humanity precisely to achieve that maturity and reciprocity of relationship which is his purpose in creation.

If salvation for the one depends on the salvation of the whole, does that not imply a form of universalism? Newbigin is naturally cautious at this point, recognizing that completion and consummation still lie in the future. He does not doubt God's purpose that all should be saved, but equally recognizes that his appeal to freedom of the will means that he cannot say that it is impossible that some will finally choose the idol rather than God, evil rather than good. Therefore, although salvation is by definition, universal and cosmic, this does not exclude the possibility that some may ultimately be 'castaways' - "To exclude this possibility would obviously be to depart completely from the gravely realistic teaching of the New Testament".[35] The claims of Jesus are absolute

---

[33] Newbigin, *Household of God*, p63.
[34] Newbigin, *Household of God*, p79.
[35] Newbigin, *Household of God*, p140.

but not irresistible. However, despite what some of his critics may think, Newbigin argues strongly that one cannot assume from this position that those who have never been presented with the chance freely to decide for or against Christ must therefore be excluded from the possibility of salvation. He recalls Jesus' reluctance to speculate on the number of those who will be saved, and stresses that in the Gospels the severest warnings about judgement and exclusion from God's presence are reserved for those who presume their own inclusion in the company of the saved. Again the emphasis is on responsibility rather than privilege:

> "The privileges to which conversion is the gateway are not exclusive claims upon God's grace; they are the privileges of those who have been chosen for special responsibility in the carrying out of God's blessed design. Their joy will be not that they are saved, but that God's name is hallowed, his will done and his reign perfected."[36]

He reiterates that to claim finality for Jesus Christ is not to assert either that the majority of people will some day become Christians, or to assert that all others will be damned. It is to claim that commitment to him is the way in which humanity can become truly aligned to the ultimate end for which all things were made.[37] Following John's Gospel, Newbigin argues that Jesus Christ is the light that enlightens *everyone* and the fundamental link between the Christian and other people is not any question of agreement or convergence between religion or ideology, but the plain fact of their common humanity.

This clear and simple theological framework for Newbigin's thought raises some important questions. If salvation is a restoration of true relationship with God and with the rest of Creation, and if this is accomplished only through the saving activity of God in Christ to which the Church bears witness, and if it is appropriated by

---

[36] Newbigin, *The Finality of Christ* (SCM London 1969), pp112-3.
[37] Newbigin, *Finality of Christ*, p115.

incorporation into the community of the people of God, how are those who do not encounter the witness of the Church to be brought into this relationship? Moreover, what of those whose experience of the reality of the Church is a denial of that true relationship for which they yearn and strive? Newbigin is clear that such folk are not necessarily consigned to perdition, but it does not seem at all obvious that he has answered his own question about how salvation becomes ours, in respect of such people.

Secondly, we must ask how adequate is Newbigin's account of human nature, especially in respect of freedom? Of course one would wish to endorse whole-heartedly his exposition of God-given freedom for true and reciprocal relationship, but does he really do justice to the bondage to which fallen human nature is subject? Are people who are presented with the testimony of the Church really free to respond positively or to reject it? How far are we bound by limitations of circumstance and culture? The balance between genuine freedom and determinism is a difficult one, but we must ask whether, for all his discussion of culture, he takes sufficient account of its strength.

Equally significant, and linking these first two points, is the question raised by his emphasis on the objectivity of the atoning work of Christ as accomplishing a new relationship between God and *the world*. If Christ has objectively achieved a new relationship in this cosmic sense, how can individuals be free to align themselves with it, or indeed to reject it? Newbigin tries to avoid this difficulty by arguing for human freedom here, but in that case it would seem that the atonement is not really as objective, either in the personal or in the cosmic sense, as he has earlier suggested.

Thirdly, and of this Newbigin was well aware, there are those within the Christian tradition who would argue that the central planks of his argument, the doctrines of the Trinity and the Incarnation, are not only potential scandals to other faiths, but culturally conditioned expressions of the Christian faith which, according to some, may well have outlived their usefulness; thus this whole question of just what the essence of the Christian message is, would not be agreed by all.

I have tried to present an outline of Bishop Newbigin's fundamental theological position. We have seen his clear conviction that the truth about human nature is to be discovered in relationship, a conviction that stems from his understanding of the nature and purpose of God as revealed in the divine action in Christ. This relational understanding is to be found in his view both of the nature of salvation and the mode by which it becomes ours through the witness of the Church. To hold this faith is to hold a clue, the vital clue, to the meaning and purpose of life itself, and to be drawn into that purpose in a responsible, free and creative manner. It is also to be commissioned to bear witness to that experience in order to widen the circle of relationship of which Christ himself is the centre and the goal. For Newbigin it is ultimately a matter of personal commitment and confession:

> "I speak of Jesus Christ as the one whom I know and confess as Lord of all that is, whom I know through the witness of the Christian tradition principally embodied in the canonical Scriptures, and whose coming to consummate all things I await."[38]

It is this personal relationship to God through Christ which is at the root of all other relationships and offers a basis for an open hospitality in which all humanity is welcome.

---

[38] Newbigin, *Christ and the Cultures* (SJT, Vol. 31 1978) pp9-10.

Chapter - 3

Our Cosmic Host: Listen in Silence

Richard Howell

Introduction

Silence is an appropriate human response when the Holy One appears on the stage of the human life.[1] This is illustrated in the message of Prophet Zechariah who calls for silence and reverence, for God purposes will be fulfilled: "Be silent, all flesh, before the LORD, for he has roused himself from his holy dwelling, (Zechariah 2:13)." Indeed the saving purposes of God were decisively fulfilled when the second person of the Holy Trinity became part of history. This is narrated in the mystery and majesty of the Virgin Mary conceiving and giving birth to "the Son of the

---

[1] The modern Quaker writer Arthur O. Roberts briefly outlines the features of silence. Roberts shows silence not as formal worship but as private reflection that nurtures the individual in the recognition of solitude. In his *Devotions on Silence* (Barclay Press, Oregon), Roberts writes that silence; 1. fosters awe before the Almighty; 2. indicates submission to God; 3. provides a posture for worship; 4. provides freedom from noise and distraction; 5. condition for tranquility; 6. sets the stage for prayer; 7. signifies respect for others; 8. renews wonder at the world; 9. provides holy space;10. prepares for effective social witness.

Most High,' (Luke 1:32) in a manger in Bethlehem, "because he will save his people from their sins (Matthew 1: 21)."

The New Testament writers bear witness in various ways to the saving acts of God as the object of faith of the Church and of all individual Christians. As a result historical Christian faith from the very beginning has confessed that God has decisively acted in the person of Jesus Christ. By decisiveness we mean the following interrelated things. First, no one can surpass Jesus in his capacity to reveal God and God's purposes for humankind. Secondly, Jesus Christ, in both his person and his work, did not merely indicate this purpose in a uniquely reliable way, he actually embodied and fulfilled it.

The servant heart of God is immediately evident in the self-emptying Christ, which speaks of a God who stoops down from on high to take his place amongst sinful human beings. As Jesus exists in a community of relations with the Father and the Holy Spirit characterized by self-emptying, so does the Church exists as a community of self-emptying presence in the world.

Mission is ontologically a defining characteristic of the church, for it expresses the inner impulse of the triune God to reveal himself, through His church in the midst of the world. God delights to make himself known, and the church is both a sign of his kingdom, pointing to the reality of God's rule of compassionate love, and a dynamic event of grace, in which God is present by His Spirit. Functionally, however, the community of faith gives form and shape to that impulse under the inspiration of the Spirit through appropriate missional engagement.

Mission refers primarily to Triune God's mission (*missio Dei*), to God's self-revelation as one who loves the world. The nature and activity of God embraces both the church and the world. Since Christians participate in the divine life, mission is at the heart of the church. Mission must be understood and interpreted as that which flows out of the corporate life of the Church. It follows from this that the task of mission is not ascribed to a few people. Mission is the responsibility of the community of God's people that reflects the collective life of the Trinity.

The role of the church is to be present in the world, because that is the arena of the Spirit's activity. The Spirit, who is the Spirit of fellowship, leading men and women into vital union with each other within the community-of-being of God himself, creates the very context within which mission takes place. To participate in the mission of Christ is to enter into the reconciling ministry of the Spirit, who is continuously at work in the world in both hidden and improbable ways, with creative innovation and resourceful ingenuity, and with concern for the particularity of context.

The Trinitarian Mission

The theological construct of *perichoresis*[2] describes the dynamic loving relations of mutuality, reciprocity and inter connectedness, which constitute the inner being of the Triune God, Father Son and Holy Spirit and provides the basis for Churches missional engagement. While we must avoid the trap of insisting that everything is mission -for then, as Stephen Neill has reminded us, "nothing is mission."[3] However we must avoid the danger of defining mission too narrowly. Bosch describes mission as "a multifaceted ministry, in respect of witness, service, justice, healing, reconciliation, liberation, peace, evangelism, fellowship, church

---

[2] John of Damascus [c. 676 – 749], who was a Syrian monk, theologian, Father of the Church, in the 8th century, used the Greek term *perichoresis* in his explanation of the text, "I am in my Father, and my Father is in me." Cf St. John Damascene on Holy Images, Followed by Three Sermons on the Assumption" –Translated by Mary H. Allies, (London, 1899).

[3] Stephen Neill, *Creative Tension*, London: Edinburgh House Press, 1959: 81.

planting, contextualization, and much more." [4] Hospitality is a key refrain to understand the mission of God.

Mission is at the heart of the Trinitarian life of God. "Because God is triune, God can bless us. Because God blesses the other in God; God can bless the other without. Because God reaches out to another already within, God is not contained by the trinity's inner life, but can reach out also to us."[5] Since Christians participate in the divine life, mission flows out of the corporate life of the Church that reflects the collective life of the Trinity.

What is the nature of the relations between divine persons; are they asymmetrical, nonegalitarian and hierarchical? To understand this Moltmann's views are important, who distinguish in the Trinity between the levels of "constitution" and the level of "life"; the one level speaks about how persons are constituted and the other about how they relate to one another. At the level of *constitution* of the divine persons, the Father is the "first" because he is the source of divinity. As John Zizioulas comments, without such a source, it would be impossible to distinguish between the three persons; they would collapse into one undifferentiated divine nature.[6] At the level of the *relations*, the Son not only "comes from" and "goes to" the

---

[4] David J. Bosch, *Transforming Mission: Paradigm Shifts in Theology of Mission* (Maryknoll, NY: Orbis, 1992), p.512. Cf. David Bosch proposes a distinction between 'mission' and 'missions'. "The first refers primarily to the missio Dei (God's mission), that is, God's self-revelation as the One who loves the world, God's involvement in and with the world, the nature and activity of God, which embraces both the church and the world , and in which the church is privileged to participate. Missions ... refer to the particular forms, related to specific times, places, or needs, of participation in the missio Dei" Ibid., p.10

[5] Rogers, Eugene F., Jr., "The Stranger as Blessing" in Buckley and Yeago, (eds), *Knowing the Triune God: The Work of the Spirit in the Practices of the Church,* (Grand Rapids; Eerdmans), 2001. p.271.

[6] John Zizioulas, *Being as Communion: Studies in Personhood and the Church.* [Crestwood: St. Vladimir's Seminary Press, 1985], p. 45.

Father, but the Father has "given all things into his hands" and "glorifies the Son" [John 13:1ff; 17:1].

With respect to the immanent Trinity, these statements about the economic Trinity mean that in constitution the Son, the Father gives all divine power and all glory to the Son. As the source of divinity the Father therefore constitutes the mutual relations between the persons as egalitarian rather than hierarchical; all persons are equal in power and equal in glory. At the level of the Trinity, the Father is not "the First," but "One among the Others".[7]

The divine persons of the Trinity do not dissolve into one another nor are they in equal. The "mutual indwelling" that results from "self giving" does not entail dissolution of the self. Instead, the self-giving is a way in which each divine person seeks the glory of the others and makes space in itself for the others. The twin notions of "self-giving" and "mutual indwelling" are the ground of belief of the coming down of the Son of God, Jesus Christ. As Volf says, this "bringing down" is the goal of the whole history of salvation.; God came into the world so as to make human beings, created in the image of God, live with one another and with God in the kind of communion in which divine persons live with one another."[8] The nature of relationships in the Trinity provides a hermeneutical principle for egalitarian male and female, family and societal relationships. This understanding of egalitarian inner Trinitarian relationships is crucial for promoting gender equality in oppressive cultures of our day.

God has revealed himself as the Lord, which means that God's very nature; ontologically and noetically is free with respect to created realities. This has important implications for multicultural communities. The belief that God is outside of any one culture

---

[7] Jurgen Moltmann, *The Spirit of Life: A Universal Affirmation*, Translated by Margaret Kohl. [San Francisco: HarperCollins, 1981], p. 308.

[8] Volf, *Exclusion and Embrace*, p. 181.

implies our allegiance is to God of all cultures. The Christian belief in the oneness of God implies God's universality, and the universality implies transcendence with respect to any given culture. The ultimate allegiance of Christians cannot be to any one culture at the same time Christians believe in the validity of all cultures. No religion can or should attempt to obliterate the cultural differences, which lie at the core of identity. At the very foundation of Christian identity lies an all encompassing change of loyalty, from a given culture with its gods to the God of all culture.

The Cosmic Host

The Triune God is the ultimate cosmic Host. The creation of human race and a wondrous variety of creatures along with this wonderful energy filled matter is God's ultimate act of hospitality. In creating the universe God made room for others. The Word of God, through whom the creation came into existence, made room for the rest of us. That same Word that later became flesh and took on the name of Jesus. In the incarnation, the One who had made space for us came down to the world he had made. But tragically, John's opening chapter tells us something else. The Word became flesh, became one of us, but when he came to his own people, his own people received him not (John 1:11). We were not at all hospitable to the One who is our ultimate Host. But isn't that just the nature of the very sin Jesus came to die for! Aren't we human beings constantly building walls, shutting people out, slamming our front door in the face of other people and other creatures?

If creation began on a note of divine hospitality, then that was meant to set the tone for the rest of all our living. In its purest sense, hospitality is sharing our home, lives, personal space, and resources without communicating a need for performance or an expectation of return. Christian hospitality reflects and participates in God's hospitality. God loves the sojourner and provides for the vulnerable. God gives the lonely a home and offers us a place at an abundant table.

In the gospels, Jesus is present as gracious host and needy guest. He welcomes the outcast and depends on the welcome of ordinary folk. In his table fellowship, he challenges cultural assumptions about who is welcome in the community and in the kingdom. Jesus identifies himself with the stranger and sick such that ministry to them is ministry to him (Matthew 25:31-46). Jesus teaches explicitly that we are to include the poor and infirm, those who seem least likely to reciprocate, in our invitations to dinner (Luke 14:12-14). We know what hospitality should look like when we dwell in and on the life of Jesus.

Our responsibility with regard to the world is therefore measured by Christian community's commitment to and solidarity with the world. This is the biblical presupposition of all Christian missions in the world. Volf rightly expresses, "If the claim that "Christ dies for the ungodly' (Romans 5:6) is the fundamental assertion of the New Testament. "While all sufferers can find comfort in solidarity of the Crucified; but only those who struggle against evil by following the example of the Crucified will discover him at their side."[9]

The Human Solidarity

The mutuality and reciprocity implicit in the intra divine life is normative as the ontological ground for all human interactions. And because all human beings are caught up with one another in the complex reality of our total environment, what Gunton calls the "bundle of life",[10] then it is appropriate to apply the periphrastic analogy inclusively rather than exclusively: it is not to be confined to the Christian community, but is relevant for all human beings. Furthermore, the richness of the language of *perichoresis* with respect

---

[9] Miroslav Volf, *Exclusion and Embrace*, (Nashville: Abingdon Press, 1996), p. 24.

[10] Colin Gunton, *The One, the Three and the Many: God, Creation and the Culture of Modernity*, Cambridge: Cambridge UP, 1993. p.170

to human community lies not only in the mutuality and reciprocity of giving and receiving, but also in its insistence that particularity is not diminished, but rather enhanced. So, as Gunton argues consistently, the concept enables 'the one and the many' in dynamic interrelations to be sustained without loss to either the particularity of the one or the plurality of the many.

The Self Moved God

As the creation of the love of God Gunton comments "the world is not a impersonal process, a machine or a self-developing organism -a cosmic collective into which the particular simply disappears - but that which itself has a destiny along with the human."[11] The distinction between God and his creation is underscored in Christian faith. "The creation of the world out of nothing is something new even for God. God was always Father, but he became Creator."[12] The new, decisive acts of God in creation, incarnation and Pentecost are indicative of the absolute and unlimited freedom of God to be other than he always has been. In ecstatic and generous love, God is neither the 'unmoved mover' of classical Aristotelian theology, nor the 'moved unmoved'[13] of process theology, but the Self-moved God who is ever open to his creation. His immutability is expressed in terms of his freedom to love, not by virtue of the static, abstract attributes implicit in classical theism. For Torrance, God is immutable because of his constancy as the ever self-living and ever self-moving Being. In ecstatic love he graces his creation with a reality and freedom of its own, authentic yet contingent upon God's own unlimited freedom.

---

[11] Gunton, Colin E., *The Promise of Trinitarian Theology*: Edinburg, T&T. Clark, 1991. P.13.

[12] Torrance, Thomas F, The Christian Doctrine of God: 222.

[13] The term 'Moved Unmover' is an expression that Torrance attributes to Colin Gunton (*Ibid.*, 239, fn. 16)

However, when *perichoresis* is applied to the Christian community of faith, it is important to recognise that human beings are not interior to the Spirit in the same way that the Spirit is interior to human beings.[14] Volf rightly observes that, in a strict sense, "there can be no correspondence to the interiority of the divine persons at a human level. Another human self cannot be internal to my own self as subject of action. Human persons are always external to one another as subjects."[15] So the indwelling of other persons is an exclusive prerogative of God.

The Spirit Creates Openness

Perichoresis is constructive at the level of the Church, the body of Christ, with respect to the interiority of personal characteristics. Each person gives of himself or herself to others, and each person in a unique way takes up others into himself or herself. This is the process of the mutual initialization of personal characteristics occurring in the church through the Holy Spirit indwelling Christians.

The Spirit opens them to one another and allows them to become catholic persons in their uniqueness. It is here that they, in a creaturely way, correspond to the catholicity of the divine persons. When the Spirit comes he creates openness in us to receive the other. Consider the transformation the Spirit brings when a person encounters Christ. Paul writes, "Therefore if anyone is in Christ, he is a new creation, the old has gone the new has come." (2 Corinthians 5:17). The Holy Spirit breaks through the self-enclosed world we dwell in and sets us on a journey with him and other members of the community of Christ.

---

[14] Volf, Miroslav, *Exclusion and Embrace*, Nashville: Abingdon Press, 1996: 182.

[15] Volf, Miroslav, *After Our Likeness: The Church as the Image of the Trinity*, Grand Rapids: Eerdmans, 1998: 208-213.

The Hospitality of the Local Church

The notion of hospitality, which informs our understanding of the inner life both of the Trinity and of the community of faith must be evident in the life of the local church fulfilling "community obligations to strangers and outsiders"[16] to bring wholeness and peace to the fragmentation and restlessness that runs through much of human life. In her collection of early Christian texts regarding hospitality and its practice, Oden traces the theme of vulnerability in five groups of people -the sick, the poor, travellers and pilgrims, widows and orphans, and slaves and prisoners. Her wide selection of texts is drawn from the first eight centuries of the Christian church and geographically covers virtually all the early Christian world. She concludes that "the pervasive character of hospitality in early Christian writing demonstrates a lack of self-consciousness, a matter-of-factness that suggests it is simply a given part of life, not the stuff of esoteric treatise."[17] So for the church today: to participate in the mission of the triune God in the world is to be willing to have our eyes opened by the Spirit of God so that we may see others "as brothers and sisters created by the same God and living as mutual guests in the same house provided by the same divine host."[18] We begin to understand God in his triune glory as we participate in his other-centred love for all people.

To participate in the mission of Christ is to enter into the reconciling ministry of the Spirit, who is continuously at work in the world both in hidden and unlikely ways. We need both the courage to look beyond our narrow evangelical and ecclesiological boundaries

---

[16] Gollings, Richard, "Planting Covenant Communities of Faith in the City" in van Engen, Charles and Tiersma, Jude (eds), *God So Loves the City: Seeking a Theology for Urban Mission*, Monrovia CA: MARC, 1994:129.

[17] Oden, Amy G. (ed), *And You Welcomed Me: A Sourcebook on Hospitality in Early Christianity*, Nashville: Abingdon Press, 2001: 27.

[18] *Ibid.*, 52.

and also the wisdom to discern where the Spirit is at work to direct all things towards the glorifying of the Son. God's particular focus on the Church has as its purpose the blessing of the nations (Gen.12:1-3; 15; 17; Isa.42:6). The Church is called to exist for the sake of its Lord and for the sake of humankind (Matt 22:32-40).

It is not the mission of the Church to choose how and when to make God known: it is the privilege and responsibility of those who confess Christ as Lord of all, to discern the will of the Father, and in obedience to respond to the Spirit who ever seeks to glorify Christ in the world. So mission is not what we do, but is determined and communicated by God's own mission of revelation and reconciliation in the world culminating in Jesus Christ and the Church. Theological reflection does not ask the question 'What would Jesus do in this situation?' because this question would imply his absence. Rather, it asks the question 'Where Jesus is in this situation and what am I to do as called by God?

In the context of bloodshed, prophet Habakkuk was astonished, that given God's goodness, holiness and universal sovereignty, how does one explain God's standing aside while the wicked swallow the righteous (1:13)? The answer came from God and is capsulated in 2:4–5. The sinner is arrogant; he will not survive. But the righteous shall live abundantly in his faithfulness. Yahweh will see to it that social structures built on violence and bloodshed will amount to nothing. But a kingdom built on the glory of God will cover the whole earth (2:14).One day all the forces opposed to God will ultimately be silenced. Habakkuk learns that God is in his holy temple, let the entire earth bow in hushed silence before him (2:20). In silence alone can we hear our Cosmic Host!

Chapter - 4

Hospitality as a Relevant Missiological Paradigm for Our Times: A Subaltern Perspective

M. Mani Chacko

Introduction

It is indeed a privilege for me to write this article in honor of my good friend and colleague Bishop D. K. Sahu, who will be celebrating his 60th birth anniversary shortly. Our friendship goes back to 1983 when we served together on the faculty of Serampore College. I am thankful for the friendship we share and hence I want to wish him all the very best as he completes 60 years of his earthly journey.

Hospitality is the relationship between guest and host, or the act or practice of being hospi

table. Specifically, this includes the reception and entertainment of guests, visitors, or strangers. *Hospitality* can also mean generously providing care and kindness to whoever is in need.In Latin; there is the word *hostis*, which means stranger, enemy. From that, we get *hospitem*, Latin for guest or host. From these roots, English gets hospital, host, hostel, hotel, hospitality. Hospitals were originally hospices for the reception of pilgrims. The term later applied to charitable institutions for the aged and infirm, and later still, to charitable institutions for the education of children, before it gained its current meaning. *Hospitallers* were those whose duty it was to provide *hospitum* (lodging and entertainment) for pilgrims. *Hospitality* was what you expected to get in a *hospital*. Thus in the current usage *Hospitality* means 'friendly reception', 'generous treatment of guests or strangers' etc.

A.   *Hospitality in the Bible*

Hospitality is given great importance both in the Old Testament and in the New Testament.

a.   *Old Testament*

God as Host. Old Testament teaching identifies the Israelites as alienated people who are dependent on God's hospitality (Psalm 39:12). God graciously received the alienated Israelites and met their needs, redeeming them from Egypt and feeding and clothing them in the wilderness (Exod 16 ; Deut 8:2-5), bringing them as sojourners into God's own land (Lev 25:23), where God offered them health, long life, peace, and fertility (Deut 11). In a figurative sense, table fellowship is offered during meals of peace offerings and religious feasts where part of the sacrifice is offered to God and the rest is eaten by the sacrificer or community (Lev 7:11-18 ; 23 Psalm 23:5 ; Prov. 9:1-6 ; Isa 25:6). Indeed, God serves as host to humanity as the one who provides food and clothing for all (Gen 1:29-30 ; 2:9 ; 3:21 ; Psalm 104:10-15 ; 136:25). God particularly cares for the alienated person (Exodus 22:22-24 ; Deut 10:17-18; Psalm 145:14-16 ; 146:9).

Israel as Host. Old Testament teaching also expected the Israelites to practice hospitality and serve as hosts, treating human life with respect and dignity. Hospitality is an act of righteous, godly behavior. When the angels journeyed to Sodom and Gomorrah in search of a righteous man, only Lot and his family were set apart to be saved. Lot was deemed righteous by the fact that he alone imitated Abraham's behavior of hospitality (Gen 19:1-8 ; 18:2-8). Besides presenting the model of Abraham, the Old Testament specifically commanded hospitality. As Israel received the loving care of Yahweh, so Israel was to love and care for the alienated person (Exod. 23:9; Lev 19:33-34; Deut 10:19; Isa. 58:6-10).

God as Guest. Another theme possibly provided an incentive for hospitality and that is God might be the guest. God or the angel of the Lord at times unexpectedly appeared in the person of the stranger (Genesis 18:1 Genesis 18:10 ; 19:1 ; Judges 6:11-24 ; 13:2-23).

b. New Testament

Jesus as Guest. Symbolically Jesus came as an alien figure to "tabernacle" in a world that did not recognize or receive him (John 1:10-14). He continues after his resurrection to offer himself as guest (Rev 3:20). On a literal level, Jesus' itinerant ministry placed him in dependence on the hospitality of others (Luke 9:58 ; 10:38). In his capacity as guest, Jesus bound himself to the lost, sharing table fellowship with tax collector, "sinner," and Pharisee alike (Mark 2:15 ; Luke 14:1 ; 19:1-10). Jesus equates himself with the needy alienated person (Matt 25:31-46).

Jesus as Host. Jesus, the guest, also becomes the host who receives an alienated world. The Old Testament allusions in the feeding of the 5, 000 (Mark 6:30-44) reveal the identity of Jesus. Taking the role of host to the multitude, Jesus is portrayed as one like Yahweh, who fed the people in the wilderness (Exod. 16); as one like the prophets of Yahweh, who fed his disciples and had food left over (2 Kings 4:42-44); as one like the coming Davidic shepherd, who would care for his flock in the wilderness (Eze 34:11-31). In the institution of the Lord's Supper, Jesus not only serves as host, washing the disciples' feet (John 13:3-5) and directing the meal, but becomes the spiritually sustaining "meal" itself (Mark 14:12-26 ; see also John 6:30-40 ; 1 Cor 10:16-17). Identifying himself with the symbolic elements of the Passover meal, Jesus associated his body with the bread of affliction that was offered to all who were hungry and needy, and he associated his blood with the cup of wine, the cup of redemption. Jesus anticipates his role as eschatological host, when he will drink again at the messianic banquet celebrating the consummation of the kingdom of God (Isa 25:6; Matt 8:11; Luke 14:15; Rev 19:9). In post resurrection appearances the disciples perceive the identity of Jesus when he takes the role of host (Luke 24:13-35; John 21:1-14).

Disciples as Guests. As persons originally alienated from God, disciples of Christ are invited to respond to Jesus as host in the celebration of the Eucharist and in anticipation of the eschatological messianic feast. Those who confess Jesus as Christ become aliens and strangers in the world (John 15:18-19; 1 Peter 1:1; 2:11). The audience of 1 Peter apparently suffered social ostracism because of their Christian confession (4:12-16), but in turn they received divine hospitality as members of the "household of God" (4:17 ; 2:9-10; Eph 2:19). Itinerant Christian ministers and refugees often found themselves in need of sympathetic hosts (Romans 16:1-2 Romans 16:23; 1 Cor 16:10-11; Titus 3:13-14; 3 John 5-8).

Disciples as Hosts. As in the Old Testament, righteous behavior in the New Testament includes the practice of hospitality. One finds the commands to act hospitably in the context of other expressions of love (Rom 12:9-21,; esp. vv. 13,20; Heb 13:1-3; 1 Peter 4:8-11; 3 John 5-8). In a general sense, disciples of Christ now serve as co-hosts with Christ to a world consisting of those who are "excluded from the citizenship in Israel and foreigners to the covenants of the promise" (Eph 2:12). Certainly, held up before the disciple is the model of Jesus, who serves as host to an alienated world, who commended hospitality in his teaching, and who himself is encountered as one who receives the alienated person (Matt 10:40; 25:31-46).

B. *Hospitality as a Relevant Missiological Paradigm for Our Times*
The existing Missiology does not bring justice to many sections of the people, therefore, we need to look for an alternative Missiology. The mission history shows the misuse of religion, especially Christianity, as an instrument or agent to protect the interest of the rich and the colonial powers. A few examples would prove the point. (a) Since the time of the first Ecumenical Council of Nicea, Christianity has consistently maintained religious legitimacy of the Empire. Hence, the Council of Nicea was convened and the Council rejected and suppressed the claims and practice of the poor Christians and established religious hegemony of the empire at that time. Gradually, faith became an obligatory state religion to express loyalty to the empire. (b) The history of Christian countries in the west shows that Christianity was used as an instrument to expand imperialism. The crusade was waged nine times by Christians against Muslims and Jews. Indigenous Christian communities were also not spared. The crusaders killed those who resisted, and destroyed and confiscated crops and properties by force. (c) The Western Christianity has been closely associated with colonial expansion. Using the military forces, Christianity was spread in Asia, Latin America and Africa. They considered colonial expansion as providence of God to bring good news to the heathen world. The colonizers not only invaded their territories, but also forcibly proselytized the people. Though some of the missionaries were critical of colonial interest, most missionaries conspired with the colonial governments and co-operated with them.

It was in this imperial historical context that Edinburgh Conference 1910 took place. The Conference was held under the patronage of colonial powers. The people who sent greetings to Edinburgh Conference included the King of England, the President of US and the rulers of colonial powers. The Edinburgh Conference clearly acknowledged that the colonial expansion was God's providence to evangelize the uncivilized and barbaric people. The Edinburgh Conference co-opted the poor and the marginalized in the scheme of Western empire. Without much alteration, we simply follow the tradition set by the Edinburgh Conference. Often mission agencies or ecumenical movements act as an agent of the empire. Mission of God should not be reduced to ruling class movement to serve the needs of the empire. It must take the position of and for the poor and must become the voice of the poor and exploited. This was greatly emphasized in the recent centenary celebrations of Ediburgh1910 held in Edinburgh from June2-6, 2010.

Under the patronage of empire, we also see a theological discourse that supports imperialism. Since the time of Constantine the Great, the theological metaphors developed in the churches supported the male rulers and oppressors. In other words, the theological concepts developed under the imperial regime not only legitimized a religion for the one who is the master and the ruler, but also sanctioned to exploit and manipulate all segments of God's creation for extraction of maximum profits. There is no place for the people who have been ruled and oppressed for centuries. We may cite three examples : (a) *The concept of God.* Theology is God-talk, discourse on God. The discourse is based on a language which is symbolic and metaphorical. Metaphors are constructed out of a cultural or social environment and context. The dominant images of God developed during the imperial power were images such as ruler, Lord, master and warrior. They are all patriarchal, political and military images. These images have made Christianity a religion of, and for the ruler, elite and the upper-class. The theological concepts or images of God which we uphold today are in deep crisis because they are not capable of liberating the poor and marginalized people from unjust system and practice. (b) *The understanding of mission.* The discourse on God as ruler and master has reinforced a success oriented or triumphalistic mission. The languages like "Mission Crusade", "Mission Campaign", "Home

Penetration", "Mass Evangelization" etc. are all military language and concepts. Christians, by and large, are engaged in denominational expansion rather than God's mission. Success in mission is measured by how many churches have been planted, converted and baptized. Mission has been very exclusive and never recognized God's revelation in other religious traditions. Mission is God's mission. God is the owner of the mission and not the churches. The churches are sent to be missionaries to witness compassion and justice with the poor and the victims. The ecumenical calling is to witness compassion and justice with the poor. But we have manipulated and acted as if we are the owners of the mission. (c) *The understanding of creation*. Western Christian interpretation of creation is anthropocentric – human is the reference point of all realities. Nature exists for human. Apart from rational beings, the other segments of God's creation cannot come under the scheme of salvation. There is no sanctity and mystery in nature, but it can be manipulated and controlled for the benefit of human beings. This one-sided theological interpretation justifies expansion of colonial power and exploitation of nature. The ideology of globalization and the expansion of global capital market are deeply rooted on this interpretation. The unprecedented exploitation of nature and present ecological crisis testify the failure of the Christian understanding of creation.

Therefore, we need a new missiological paradigm where God is perceived as a fellow sufferer, a great comforter, divine power not as a dominating or controlling power nor as dialectical power in weakness but as liberating and transforming power that is effective in compassionate love, care and service. We need a radical departure from the imperial theology of the missionary movement because their Christian values are used to support rulers and oppressors, and perpetuate an unmindful exploitation of earth's resources.

There is an imbalance in the acknowledgement of the richness of theologies of the marginalized – the dalits, the tribals, and adivasis, which are accorded secondary status both in Theology and the Mission of the church. Indigenous people demand the right to respect their culture, spirituality, language, tradition, forms of organization, ways of knowing and doing, and their intellectual properties. There is a need for the Church to go outside the walls of its institutional network and to tap the energy and vitality that exists beyond its present partnership boundaries.

Similar thinking process is being carried forward by theologians dealing with subaltern issues and one of them is Rev. Y. T. Vinayaraj, a Presbyter of the Mar Thoma Church. His words are worthy of note: *Modern Christian mission was the mission to 'the lost sheep'. Sociologically speaking, the mission envisaged by colonial modernity was empowerment programmes in order to 'lift up' the 'weak' and the 'vulnerable' to the modern/civilized/developed civil life. Thus we had the 'missions' to Africans/Afro-Americans/Asians etc. Of course this has impacted changes in the life worlds of the missionized people, but on the other hand, it neglected their social agency for engaging to re-draw their own subjectivity, social space and social status. It was an empowerment programme. Empowerment is always a programme from outside while the internal discourses, habitus, practices and episteme remain intact.*

*The whole historical meta narra*tives of the modern missionaries and mission agencies were reports of their sacrificial work among the 'uncivilized people'…The time has come to re-read these colonial 'missiological meta narratives' and create new 'little'/ 'local' conversion stories of the so-called 'missiological other'… Today the 'missiological other' has become capable enough to de-construct their subjectivity and social agency. Thus mission in the modern sense has become impossible. In the postmodern sense mission is everywhere and not to be focused in a particular region or culture or people. It can be 'from everywhere to every where'. There is a hermeneutical imperative to attend the plural-local life affirming engagements or resistances of the subalterns in order to acknowledge and recognize the political/ epistemological differences of the plural life worlds. Thus the mission as it is envisaged in the project of modernity has become impossible today due to the death of the 'missiological other'... The mission in the postmodern sense is an invitation to a kind of hospitality where both the 'host' and the 'stranger' deconstructs each other and finds a renewed status mutually by celebrating their rights to be different. It is an invitation to enter in to a renewed understanding of relationship. It is the responsibility for the other, being for the other. It is an invitation to engage with new imaginations, new relationships, new practices and new dialogues of fraternity. The unity that neglects the dignity of the difference is hegemonic. It is in the differences that we find our potentialities and strength. All the subaltern movements are to be located in their own specificities and particularities. Dalit itself is a plural category where we particularly attend the issues of Dalit women and children.

Thus treating Dalits or Tribals or Women as a collective/ essentialist/ unitary category and creating solidarity programmes while keeping the paternalist consciousness, seems untenable today. In the changed theoretical-theological-epistemological context, 'solidarity' means a re-imagination of ourselves; not mere a sense of 'standing along with' or 'speaking for' or 'representing somebody'. It is not just the burden of constituting some slogans for the transformation of the 'other', while keeping ourselves intact. It is a new journey of re-looking our own faith, tradition, theology and ontology. Thus doing theology means reconstituting our own ontology and theology. Christian faith is a total commitment to the ongoing journey of finding 'our-selves' dialogically and transforming our life-world theologically... Thus, in the postmodern context theological locatedness is very important. Who is speaking for whom gets importance here. This is the hermeneutical importance of the particular theologies like Dalit/tribal/feminist theologies in the changed epistemological context (Re-defining Oikoumene: A Subaltern Perspective)

Conclusion

The subaltern communities are no longer objects to be evangelized. They are rather subjects in the conversations on Mission of God. Their role as subjects should find an adequate space in our missiology. There is no longer the "missiological other" as Vinyaraj eloquently argues. The subaltern communities are active social agents of a democratic society with their own stories and communal practices. They are overcoming their long-standing oppressed consciousness. Indigenous peoples of all continents are rediscovering the wisdom and life affirming values of their own cultures. They thus are active players in the mission of God, conversations and activities. It is here "Hospitality" becomes a relevant missiological paradigm for our times.

Chapter - 5

The Theology of Inculturation Re-examined

K.P. Aleaz

This paper is submitted in honour of my friend D. K. Sahu, theologian and bishop, wishing him all the best in all the days to come. It is divided into four sections. The first section is on a theological framework for Inculturation. The second section provides a further interpretation of Inculturation. The relative merit of the term Inculturation as well as the evolution of its meaning in the Church is taken note of in this section. The third section gives a brief picture of the various attempts in the Church for Inculturation. In the fourth section the views of some theologians evaluating Inculturation are looked into. The last section provides some concluding observations.

1.   The Theological Framework

a.   *Inculturation is Christianization*

The Gospel is not identical with culture; rather it is independent in regard to all cultures. But the Kingdom which the Gospel proclaims is lived by people who are very much linked to a culture and so building up of the Kingdom involves borrowing the elements of human cultures. Though independent of cultures, the Gospel is not incompatible with it; rather it is capable of permeating all cultures without becoming subject to any of them.[1] Cultures have to be regenerated by an encounter with the Gospel; every effort has to be made for a full evangelization of cultures. Consequently, in the Indian context, Inculturation is not Hinduisation but Christianization.[2]

In Inculturation "some elements from Hinduism are taken and purified, given a new interpretation and integrated into Christian ... life".[3] In Inculturation elements from other religions are subjected to a Christian scrutiny and interpretation, rejecting false doctrines, superstitions and all forms of sin and evil. "Nothing can be integrated into our theology, liturgy, and spirituality unless they have values in them, unless they can survive a prophetic critique, unless they acquire a Christian meaning.... This is an important and indispensable condition for inculturation". The words of Christ are words of judgment and grace. This fact holds good for the various goods of this world which bear the mark of both human's sin and of God's blessings (AG 8b). Whatever good is found in the hearts and minds of humans, or in the rites and cultures peculiar to various people is not lost. It is healed, ennobled and perfected (AG 9C. Cf. LG 17).

Inculturation supposes participation in the paschal mystery or the process of redemptive incarnation, death, resurrection and glorification; and the mystery of the Church is also analogically modelled upon this. The Church should continue to live the paschal

---

[1] D. S. Amalorpavadass, "Indian Culture. Integrating Cultural Elements into our Spirituality" in Indian *Christian Spirituality* ed. by D. S. Amalorpavadass, Bangalore: NBCLC, 1982, p. 100.

[2] D. S. Amalorpavadass, in *Indian Christian Spirituality* ed. by D. S. Amalorpavadass, *op. cit.*, p. 109-110.

[3] *Ibid.*, pp. 109-110.

mystery, i.e., should get incarnated in local cultures, should die to sin and resurrect to liberation and new creation. The Church's mission is to make all conform to Christ and the same holds good for inculturation.[4] The doctrines and practices of other religions are to be brought to the touchstone of Christ and his paschal mystery. They should be first made to pass through Christ's death and resurrection.[5]

b.   Theological bases of Inculturation

After creating, God said 'it is good' (Gen.1.25) and this implies the fact that Creation is the manifestation of the love of God in all created realities. In the Word of God were created all things in heaven and on earth, everything visible and invisible (Jn.1.3). Vatican II affirms that the seeds of the word are found in all religions and temporal realities (AG2). Such an understanding of the world is the first step in inculturation.[6] Secondly, the transformation of the world is effected in Christ through a process of inculturation understood as incarnation; the theology of redemption i.e., incarnation, death and resurrection points to the path of inculturation.[7] Thirdly, the Church continues the mission of Christ. It is through the process of incarnation that the Church comes into existence in a place; the Church becomes localized and concretized in human community. The Church proclaims the word to the human community which transforms it and it expresses this transformation through structures taken from its own cultural heritage. It should be noted that inculturation is something beyond acculturation. It is our human response to the faith, a free and spontaneous response rooted in the

---

[4] *Ibid.*, p.110; Paul Puthanangady, *op.cit.*, pp. 103-104.

[5] D. S. Amalorpavadass, *Ibid.*, pp. 110-111.

[6] Joseph Prasad Pinto, Inculturation through Basic Communities, Bangalore: ATC, 1985, pp. 23-25; Paul Puthanangady, *op.cit.*, p.103; D. S. Amalorpavadass, *op.cit.*, Bangalore: NBCLC, 1978, pp. 17-18.

[7] Julian Saldanha, *Inculturation*, Bombay: St. Paul's Publications, 1987, pp. 39-41.

local culture. It is an encounter between faith and culture. Therefore nobody can decide any framework or fix a pattern for the process of inculturation

c.   *Areas of Inculturation*

D. S. Amalorpavadass has listed the following sixteen areas of Inculturation:[8] i) Language, literature. ii) Basic knowledge of cultures and religions of the region.iii) Sociological inculturation (social customs, dress, food, habitation, major events of life, birth, marriage, funerals). iv) Incarnation among the people; identification with them; insertion into the mainstream of national life: socio-political, cultural and religious.v) Arts (dance, drama, music, painting, decoration, sculpture, architecture). vi) Liturgy and Prayer/Meditation. vii) Spirituality: sadhanas and margas.viii) Theology.ix) Religious life.x) Formation of clergy, religious and lay people.xi) Indigenous forms of preaching or faith-education.xii) Ministries and services. xiii) Organization, institutions and structures.xiv) Indigenous leadership.xv) Self-reliance in finance and other sources. xvi) Life-style.

Inculturation has to happen in the 'great tradition' as well as 'little tradition' of every culture. In India inculturation has been mainly around the great or Sanskritic traditions of the Indian society and credit goes to liberation theologies such as Dalit and Tribal theologies for having turned the attention of the Church to the lower strata of the society.[9] Faith is lived, clothed, enveloped, and expressed in a culture and the problem of inculturation today is with regard to the imposition of the Western Latin cultural form the Church has acquired during the course of history, upon people who have a different culture.[10] What is needed is not levelling all differences by

---

[8] D. S. Amalorpavadass, in *Indian Christian Spirituality, op.cit.,* p.101.

[9] Cf. L. Lobo, "Towards an Inculturation in the Non-Sanskritic Traditions" *Vidyajyoti,* Vol. 49, 1985, pp. 16-28.

[10] Y. Congar, "Christianity as Faith and as Culture", *East Asian Pastoral Review,* Vol. 18, 1981, pp. 304-319.

extending the Latin and European form of faith-culture to all countries and people, but to establish unity in diversity by the realization of the universal faith in the particular cultures. We should be able to distinguish between the accidentals and essentials of the already inculturated Christian message.

d.   The Significance of the Cultures

The Gospel has to be rooted in the local cultures and so cultures are important. The Vatican II says: 'The seed which is the word of God sprouts from the good ground watered by divine dew. From this ground the seed draws nourishing elements which it transforms and assimilates into itself. Finally it bears much fruit (AG 22). 'From the seed which is the word of God, particular Churches can be adequately established and flourish the world over, endowed with their own vitality and maturity' (AG 6e). 'Thus the congregation of the faithful endowed with the riches of its own nation's culture, should be deeply rooted in the people' (AG 15d).[11]

Christ is present in the Church, but one cannot identify Christ with the Church. Also, the Kingdom is present in the Church, but the Church and the Kingdom are not identical. The Church is a contingent, historical, temporary and relative realization. So many elements of truth can be found outside the Church and these have dynamism towards Catholic unity, which is accomplished through inculturation. "Many elements of sanctification and truth can be found outside of her visible structure. These elements, however as gifts properly belong to the Church of Christ, possess an inner dynamism towards Catholic unity" (LG 8).[12]

2.   An Interpretation of Inculturation

Words such as 'adaptation', 'accommodation', and 'indigenization' were used in the past to express the encounter between the Christian

---

[11] D. S. Amalorpavadass, in *Indian Christian Spirituality, op. cit.*, p. 113.
[12] *Ibid.*, pp. 112-113.

message and different cultures. It was the term 'adaptation' which was most widely used in the past. The word indigenous is related to a nature metaphor, i.e., of the soil. The limitation of this term may be that it is past-oriented and so cannot express the dynamic changing aspect of culture. The term 'contextualization' which is more often used among Protestants can convey all that is implied in 'indigenization' as well as a dynamic aspect which is, future oriented and open to change.[13] 'Acculturation' is the anthropological term which signifies inter-cultural contact resulting in changes in the original cultural patterns of either one group or both groups of people. 'Enculturation' is another less used anthropological term meaning the gradual process by which an individual achieves competence in his/her own culture.

The term inculturation[14] was introduced by J. Masson in 1962 to signify a process by which Church becomes inserted in a given culture. Jesuit study circles and documents use this term popularly since 1974. The Federation of Asian Bishop's Conference used the term in 1974. The Pastoral Constitution on the Church in the Modern World, *Gaudium et Spes* of Vatican II has a full chapter on the proper development of culture. The plurality of cultures is admitted with equal respect and we are encouraged to share it in various forms.[15] The Decree on the missions, *Ad Gentes* expounds the Church's new understanding of mission which has an openness to all that is good in every culture and religion. The document proposes the mystery of the Incarnation as the model for inculturation of the Church in different cultures.[16] According to the *Encyclical Letter Redemptoris Missio* of Pope John Paul II on the Permanent Validity of the Church's Missionary Mandate, Rome, 7th December 1990, inculturation is not mere external adaptation but intimate

---

[13] *Ibid.*, p. 10.
[14] *Ibid.*, pp. 11-12.
[15] *Ibid.*, p. 63.
[16] *Ibid.*, pp. 63-64.

transformation of authentic cultural values through their integration in Christianity and the insertion of Christianity in the various human cultures; the church takes in the good elements existing in different cultures renewing them from within in terms of the principles of compatibility with the Gospel and communion with the universal Church.[17]

3.   Inculturation in the Church

a.   *Efforts for Inculturation in the Two Third World Countries*

The National Biblical Catechetical and Liturgical Centre at Bangalore played a significant role in inculturation in the Post-Vatican II period. Initially Latin American theology offered resistance and hesitated to accept culture as part of the analysis of reality. It considered the socio-economic aspects as the main cause of poverty and oppression and hence cultural elements were seen as a consequence of these. But EATWOT (Ecumenical Association of Third World Theologians) Conferences influenced Latin American perspective to realize the need to include religion and culture in the work of social analysis.[18] The Puebla Document brought out by the Third General Conference of the Latin American Episcopate in 1979, which has a whole section on evangelization and culture, speaks about evangelical renewal and transformation of Latin American culture; the Gospel must penetrate the values and criteria that inspire culture, so that people can become fully human.[19] Pope John Paul II in his addresses in Africa in 1980 and 1982 has tried to interrelate Gospel and culture. According to him

---

[17] Encyclical Letter Redemptoris Missio of the Supreme Pontiff, John Paul II Rome, 7th December 1990, pp. 89-93.

[18] Sergio Torres Gonzalez, "The Inculturation of the Gospel in Latin American Continent" in Third World Theologies in Dialogue. Bangalore: EATWOT, 1991, pp. 19-28.

[19] Joseph Prasad Pinto, *Inculturation through Basic Communities. An Indian Persepective, op.cit.*, p.69.

one of the aspects of evangelization is the inculturation of the Gospel and the Africanization of the Church. It is on the path of culture that humans encounter Christ who embodies the values of all cultures.

b. *Inculturation in India*

The Roman Catholic Church in India has taken certain positive measures in the sphere of inculturation in worship, and life-style after the IInd Vatican Council. .[20] To begin with, from the early 70s attempts were made to create an Indian atmosphere of worship, consisting chiefly of postures, gestures, objects and elements in the liturgy, vestments etc. An Indian Anaphora was prepared and this was approved by the Catholic Bishop's Conference of India (CBCI) in 1972. The Anaphora affirmed God's presence in the whole creation. It refers to the invitation offered to humans to share in the life of Saccidananda. The cosmic covenant is applied to the Indian context by referring to the search for God as Power present in the Primal Religions, search for God in Hinduism through the karma, bhakti and jnana margas. Mention is made also of Buddhism, Jainism, and Islam. Since the CBCI meeting in 1970 scriptures of other religions and Indian religious literature were used in liturgy and the Research Seminar on non-Biblical Scriptures organized by National Biblical Catechetical and Liturgical Centre (NBCLC), Bangalore in 1974 was an immensely encouraging step.[21] Prayer and meditation through Christian Yoga and Indian type of Ashrams were encouraged.

But after the intervention of the Prefect of the Congregation for Divine Worship forbidding the use of the Indian Anaphora, the CBCI has shown excessive caution in the matter of inculturation.[22]

---

[20] Cf. Julian Saldanha, *Inculturation, op.cit.,* pp. 47-83.

[21] *Ibid.,* pp. 109-110. Cf. D. S. Amalorpavadass (ed.), *eminar on Non-Biblical Scriptures,* Bangalore: NBCLC, 1974.

[22] Paul Puthenangady, "Liturgical Inculturation in India", *Jevadhara,* Vol. XXIII, No. 135, May 1993, p. 200.

It should be pointed out that the meeting of the Bishops of the Latin Rite in India has always encouraged liturgical inculturation in India.[23] Since 1979 when regional autonomy for inculturation was given in India by the CBCI, North Indian region worked seriously towards the inculturation of liturgy, while the Southern region continued in their traditional liturgical practice.[24] Since 1987 when India was constituted into three Individual Churches by the Pope, liturgical matters came under each Ritual Church. In the 1991 meeting of the Conference of the Catholic Bishops of India (CCBI)-Latin, a revised text of the forbidden Anaphora was presented and approved. At the level of Catechisms inculturation is encouraged in India; inculturated books on Catechism 'God-with-us series' are making headway not only in the plains, but also in the Tribal areas of Chota Nagpur and North East

4.   A Theological Evaluation of Inculturation

a.   *Understanding and Interpretation of the Gospel*

It is the hermeneutical context or the contextual socio-politico-religio-cultural realities which decide the content of our knowledge and experience of the Gospel. Knowledge is formulated in the very knowing process and understanding the Gospel of God in Jesus is a continuous integrated non-dual divine-human process. Nothing is pre-given or pre-formulated. There is nothing pre-given or pre-formulated by somebody which can then be incultured, indigenized, adapted or contextualized... Inculturation of the pre-formulated gospel is an unreality.[25] The hermeneutical principle implied in the theological position that first there is some readymade piece of precious knowable material given to humans and then we undertake the hard work of understanding it, is unconvincing. In reality,

---

[23] *Ibid.*, pp. 201-202.

[24] *Ibid.*, p. 201.

[25] K. P. Aleaz, *The Gospel of Indian Culture*, Calcutta: Punthi Pustak, 1994, pp. 177-282.

knowledge does not happen in that way. In reality there is no gap between the knower, the knowledge and the object known. Knowledge of anything is an immediate existential knowledge of the thing by the knower; the content of knowledge itself is formulated in the very knowing process. The same defective hermeneutical principle we may notice being implied in the current theological concepts of Inculturation, Indigenization, Adaptation and Contextualization. These concepts also imply a duality between the knower and the knowledge and between the knower and the object known. But in our understanding process there exists nothing externally ready made that can be incultured, indigenized, adapted or contextualized. Whatever we know and experience is being constructed in the very knowing process.[26]

The theological constructions of Indian thinkers such as Brahmabandhav Upadhyaya, P. Chenchiah and K. Subbha Rao further ratify this point. Brahmabandhav Upadhyaya was of the view that the Vedantic conception of God and that of Christian belief are exactly the same and that Maya of Advaita Vedanta is the best available concept to explain the doctrine of creation. Upadhyaya did not reinterpret either of the Vedantic concepts Saccidananda and Maya, to serve as the explanations of a ready made Christian theology. Rather he showed that Saccidananda is Trinity and that Maya expresses the meaning of the doctrine of creation in a far better way than the Latin root *Creare*.[27] P. Chenchiah discovered the supreme value of Christ not in spite of Hinduism but because Hinduism had taught him to discern spiritual greatness. For him theology was based on direct experience of Jesus and this experience varies as per the background and context of the believer. Hence, there is a possibility for new interpretations of Jesus. His own

---

[26] K. P. Aleaz, *An Indian Jesus from Sankara's Thought*, Calcutta: Punthi Pustak, 1977, p. 15.

[27] K. P. Aleaz, *Christian Thought through Advaita Vedanta, op. cit.*, pp.9-38.

experience was that, Christianity is not primarily a doctrine of salvation but the announcement of the advent of a new creative order in Jesus namely, the Kingdom of God where the cosmic energy or Shakti is the Holy Spirit. We are incorporated in the new creation of Jesus today through the Yoga of the Yoga of the Holy Spirit, which is in line with the integral Yoga of Sri Aurobindo.[28] Kalagara Subha Rao was of the view that in following Jesus the Gurudev, our foundation has to be Jesus Christ alone, beyond doctrines and rituals; and he gave expression to his experience in confronting Jesus through Advaita Vedantic categories. Jesus died to the body and ego through self-sacrifice and he calls us to follow his way through his grace. We are in reality spirit, ignorance (*ajnana*) of this fact makes us the servant of the body and that is Fall and the fallen state is sin. Jesus leads us from *ajnana* to *jnana* (knowledge); form the material realm to the spiritual realm.[29]

b.   The Limitations of Inculturation as a Theological Method

The act of theologizing is more than Indigenization or Inculturation. Christopher Duraisingh explains: "The act of theologizing is not what we often call indigenization, that is, indigenizing something that is alien and external to our context: the concept of indigenization must be carefully examined and exposed as a concept that seems to suggest that the Gospel is external and alien to us and that by our effort we can acclimatize or indigenize it... Instead, we must be able to speak of interiorizing the Gospel in such a way that the meaning of the Gospel, which transcends both what we and the text bring to the moment of encounter, emerges from within, addressing us, transforming us and bringing into being something

---

[28] Cf. G. V. Job, P. Chenchiah et al., *Rethinking Christianity in India*, Madras: A. N. Sundarisanam, 1938.

[29] K. P. Aleaz, *Christian Thought through Advaita Vedanta, op.cit.*, pp. 45-62.

wholly new".[30] Underlying the concepts like indigenization, contextualization and inculturation, there seems to be the notion of a false dichotomy between message and context. We should note that the message is always apprehended together with the acquired structure of consciousness given in a context. Language and human apprehension arise together in the mind's act. This is true of the theology of the Church Fathers as well as Indian Christian theology.

According to A. P. Nirmal there is no such word as 'indigenize' in the verbal form and therefore the usual expression 'indigenization' is linguistically untenable.[31] "Someone or something either is indigenous or not. 'Indigenization' therefore, is a contradiction in terms. It is an attempt – an artificial attempt – to make indigenous that which is not indigenous". 'Indigenization' of the gospel implies the wrong notions that the gospel is something foreign, Christian theology is translation of the Christian faith into a given situation and the gospel as well as history is static. Further, theologically indigenization would be a denial of the basic Christian theological affirmation that God is the Creator of the whole universe. "'Indigenization' really means first of all the branding of God as a 'foreigner' in his own home and then having branded him a 'foreigner', seeking to make him 'indigenous' in our own country, nation, culture and so on". God as always indigenous to India as to any other country and his indigeneity has a salvific purpose. Hence "the task of any indigenous theology is not to seek to indigenize a god who is a foreigner, but rather to seek to understand God who is indigenous to any given situation and is savingly active in the dynamics of a given history.

---

[30] Christopher Duraisingh, "Reflections on Theological Hermeneutics in the Indian Context', in *The Indian Journal of Theology*, Vol. 31, Nos. 3 and 4, July-Dec. 1982, pp.266-67.

[31] Arvind P. Nirmal, "Theological Implications of the Term 'Indigenous'" in *Dialogue in Community. Essays in Honour of S. J. Samartha*, ed. by C.D. Jathanna, Mangalore: Karnataka Theological Research Institute, 1982, p.169.

c.   *A Few Negative Points of Inculturation*

There are theologians who think that Oriental spirituality which stands for the positive pole of Asian religion, for the whole way of being and seeing that one acquires when the inner core of one's personality is radically transformed by means of an asceticism of renunciation, should become the locus of an indigenous theology.[32] But here we must be careful to avoid the 'theological vandalism' by which, all too often, Oriental techniques of introspection are pulled out of the soteriological ethos of Eastern religions and made to 'serve' Christian prayer with no reverence for the wholeness of the religious experience of people of other faiths.[33] Also, "any tendency to create or perpetuate a 'leisure class' through 'prayer centers' and 'ashrams' that attract the more affluent to short spells of mental tranquillity rather than to a life of renunciation is an abuse of Oriental spirituality"[34] and hence should be avoided. There are people in India whose evaluation of the inculturation and theologizing taking place in some Indian Christian Ashrams is that it is not inculturation but imposture as what is involved is slavish imitation of brahminical rituals, brahminical regulations of diet, Hindu techniques of prayer etc.[35] At the same time there are still some who talk about the need to draw from a deep Asian experience where proclamation and dialogue which are the two dimensions of the mission, are lived as an integral whole.[36] Others say if "Oriental spirituality is endorsed in Christian circle as an *apolitical escape* from complex human situations, rather than allow to burst forth as a *prophetic movement*

---

[32] Aloysius Pieris, *An Asian Theology of Liberation*, Maryknoll: Orbis Books, 1988, p. 41.

[33] *Ibid.*, pp. 41-42.

[34] *Ibid.*, p. 42.

[35] Cf. George M. Soares Prabhu, "From Alienation to Inculturation" in *Bread and Breath*, ed. by T. K. John, Anand: Gujarat Sahitya Prakash, 1991, pp.55-99.

[36] Michael Amladoss, "Proclaiming the Gospel", *Vidyajyoti*, Vol. 57, No. 1, January 1993, pp. 26-32.

against the organized sin that keeps Asian poor"[37] the Church must put an end to such endorsement.

d. Not Inculturation but Enreligionization or Interculturation is the Need

In the opinion of the Church fathers only the culture of Rome and the philosophy of Greece were worth being adapted by the church. In other words the Church stood for a separation of religion from culture (as in Latin Christianity) and religion from philosophy (as in Hellenistic Christianity) and thus propagated a 'Christ-against-religion theology'. But this sort of a separation of religion from culture and philosophy does not make sense in Asian society. Aloysius Pieris makes his point clear that the very word 'inculturation' which is of Catholic origin and inspiration, is based on this culture-religion dichotomy of the Latins, in that it could, and often does, mean the insertion of 'the Christian religion minus European culture' into an 'Asian culture minus non-Christian religion'.[38]

In the Asian context we cannot separate a philosophy or culture from its soteriological religious content. The Greek manner of instrumentalizing philosophy and the Latin practice of instrumentalizing a non-Christian culture, becomes a 'theological vandalism' in Asia.[39] When we receive for example 'Buddhist techniques' of meditation in 'Christian prayer' we have to take into account the soteriological context of such techniques; the Buddhist way and Buddhist truth go side by side; method cannot be severed from goal.[40] The Church has truncated Asian culture and philosophy from their religious context and then used these against Asian religions, to baptize Asian religiousness and to convert people from Asian religions. This is nothing but Christian triumphalism

---

[37] Aloysius Pieris, *An Asian Theology of Liberation, op. cit.*, p.42.
[38] *Ibid.*, p.52.
[39] *Ibid.*, p.53.

which has no reverence for the wholeness of the religious experience of others.[41] Perhaps, it is high time that we come to the realization that inculturation is not a religiously neutral act.

5. Conclusion

Cultures are regenerated by an encounter with the Gospel. Inculturation supposes participation in the paschal mystery; religions and cultures are to pass through Christ's death and resurrection. The doctrines of Creation, Incarnation/Redemption and the Church are the theological bases of Inculturation. All creation is by the Word of God. God found the creation to be good. The seeds of the Word are in all creatures. The Incarnation of Christ was inculturation. The theology of redemption i.e., incarnation, death and resurrection points to the path of inculturation. The Church continues the mission of Christ through incarnation in a local situation; she interprets the mysteries of the Kingdom through the local cultural forms. A genuine process of inculturation facilitates a synthesis of faith and culture; faith purifies culture and culture helps faith to diffuse socially through art, poetry, philosophy and the like. Inculturation has to be effected in all the realms of the life of the Church such as liturgy, spirituality, theology, ministries, institutions and so on.

It is claimed that Inculturation signifies both external and internal changes as well as a deep sense of belonging to the culture with its past, present and future dynamism. Inculturation is not mere external adaptation but intimate transformation of authentic cultural values through their integration in Christianity and the insertion of Christianity in the various human cultures. Inculturation has to be guided by the twin principles of compatibility with the Gospel and communion with the universal Church. The Christian message supports many values found and lived in various cultures, but at the same time may put in question some culturally accepted values. Through inculturation the Christian message becomes not only intelligible to the local people but it also becomes conceived as responding to their deepest aspiration.

The National Biblical Catechetical and Liturgical Centre (NBCLC) in Bangalore played an important role in Inculturation in the post-Vatican II period. The EATWOT (Ecumenical Association of Third World Theologians) Conferences influenced Latin American perspective to realize the need to include religion and culture in the work of social analysis. The African Church is for the inculturation of the Gospel and Africanization of the Church. Various attempts were made in India for liturgical inculturation. An Indian Anaphora was prepared and this was approved by the CBCI (Catholic Bishop's Conference of India) in 1972; but later the Prefect of the Congregation for Divine Worship disallowed the use of this anaphora. In 1991 a revised text of this anaphora was approved by the CCBI (Conference of the Catholic Bishop's of India)-Latin. Bishops of the Latin Rite are encouraging inculturation; in the North India region inculturation is being taken seriously.

There is a view among some thinkers in India that the inculturation taking place in some Christian Ashrams is nothing but imposture as what is involved is slavish imitation of brahminical traditions in rituals, diet, techniques of prayer etc. If we pull oriental techniques of introspection out of the soteriological ethos of Eastern religions, we will be committing 'theological vandalism'. 'Oriental spirituality' should not be conceived as an *apolitical escape* rather it has to be allowed to burst forth as a *prophetic movement*. Separation of religion from culture and philosophy does not make sense in Asian society. So in Christian triumphalism if inculturation means the insertion of 'the Christian religion minus European culture' into an 'Asian culture minus non-Christian religion', that is an impossibility. In Asia what is needed is, not just inculturation but *enreligionization* or *interculturation*. Because cultural incursions have religious consequences and mutual fecundation is what is desirable in the dialogical experience of religious pluralism.

Non-Roman Catholic Indian theologians also have exposed the defects of the concepts like Indigenization, Adaptation, Contextualization or Inclturation. These concepts imply the following misconceptions: The Gospel is external and alien to us; revising the language of the unchanging Gospel is what is needed; there is a dichotomy between message and context; and we can judge our religious tradition from inside and those of others from outside. We should always remember that Indian Christian consciousness is co-constituted by the Judeo-Christian tradition and elements of our pan-Indian heritage through their continuous confluence. In the understanding and interpretation process there is nothing pre-given or pre-formulated by somebody which then can be indigenized, adapted, contextualized or incultured. At the same time, in the understanding and interpretation process there is always the possibility of the emergence of the new in Christian thought and this is not conceived in Indigenization, Adaptation, Contextualization or Inculturation. Indigenization is a contradiction in terms because it is an artificial attempt to make indigenous that which is not indigenous. It implies Christian theology which is foreign has to be translated in India. Theologically it is also branding God the Creator as a foreigner to our country and culture. We should not forget that God and Christian theology are always indigenous in our country.

Chapter - 6

Theological Education in India: Concerns and Reflections

Ravi Tiwari

Preliminaries

To attain something in life is a time for celebration, more so, if it is a landmark in life. Being a member of Hexa-fold club was considered an achievement in itself from the ancient of days in India; it qualified a person to be known as a wise-man in the community. There is no doubt the DK (as I have always known him) deserves to be so. I am sure, the experiences in life, and the knowledge he acquired in academia, have also added to this status. I have known DK since 1982; we taught together at Serampore and he was my neighbour for some time. We shared many a vision together, fought together over common issues and concerns; so also fought against each other if we had divergent interests or policies. In-spite of ups and downs in life our friendship and relation never soured or broken. We surely went our own ways, but kept our line of communication in tact. Most of DK's life, like mine, was spent in theological education; this has been our commitment, and our main interest. At this time, celebrating with him the gift of life, I wish to pay my tribute to DK through this humble reflection on some aspects of theological education.

Introduction

Senate of Serampore College (University) (SSC) and the Board of Theological Education of Senate of Serampore College (BTESSC) normally meet once a year to take stock of the year and decide on policy matters. There are more than hundred members in BTESSC which acts as an advisory body to the Senate. BTESSC helps the Senate to take decisions, in the interest of the church and society, on academic matters. BTESSC is more representative body as its members are the principals of affiliated colleges, church leaders, institutions engaged in theological education, staff and student representatives from affiliated institutions. Senate has eighteen members and is responsible for academic management and administration of Serampore College as a university which, at present, conduct examination process for the Faculty of Theology of the university.

There are a few partners and fraternity friends who attend these meetings as invitees. Ecumenical Theological Education of World Council of Churches (ETE-WCC) has been one of the long-time partners and supporter of the Senate and theological education in India. It is a matter of great satisfaction that its representative has always made a point to be with the BTESSC during its annual meetings. Dr. Dietrich Werner as the Director of ETE-WCC attended the Senate and BTESSC meetings recently held at United Theological College, Bangalore from February 3-6, 2010. He sent some of his reflections to me as the Registrar of the Senate, on the matters of mutual concerns for theological education in India, and I responded to them. It is presented here in the form of dialogue between us.

The Dialogue

Dr. Dietrich Werner (DW): Many thanks for having invited me to the meetings of BTESSC and Senate of Serampore College in

Bangalore and the following convocation ceremony. It again provided an excellent opportunity to be in touch with the excellent work you are doing and the manifold challenges and exciting new reforms which Indian theological education is facing and undertaking today. I have been in touch with many of the present representatives in personal encounters and discussions and had the feeling that the presence of ETE was valued as a sign of interest, solidarity and continued accompaniment. Many follow up tasks in terms of networking and requests have evolved from individual contacts.

I hope that the "world study report on theological education 2009" which I distributed can serve as a tool to enable Indian theological education to take part in some of the debates and crucial challenges theological education is facing also in other parts of the world. The electronic version of this document can be downloaded from our website or from the website of Edinburgh centenary conference for which this is prepared for.

I am glad that ETE can continue to work for the next two years, though I have shared with you and others that WCC facing huge financial challenges in the years ahead is also reshaping its mode of operation – particularly in the area of grant-giving – in a consultative processes with its partners. Senate of Serampore members will be closely involved in the processes planned accordingly this year in ways we discussed during the Bangalore meetings (WOCATI Executive Meeting in Edinburgh June 2010 with Dr. James Massey; ETE Accompaniment Group and Asian Partners Meeting with Dr. Wati Longchar in April and July this year).

Dr. Ravi Tiwari (RT): ETE-WCC has been an important partner of SSC since last many years and we always value their partnership. It was unfortunate that SSC could not be accommodated in much of its programmes and consultations, and a distinction was made between SSC and the Board (BTESSC). Senate is responsible for academics whereas BTESSC is responsible for relations with the churches and other bodies engaged in theological education.

DW: I am fully aware of the different functions between the Senate being responsible for the academic issues and BTESSC which related to issues of mutual interest between churches and theological colleges. I ask for your forgiveness that I did not properly associate the concerns raised to either of them, being aware that some issues might be more in the area of the one, others in the other.

RT: I am sure; we will continue to work with proper understanding and with spirit of cooperation for strengthening the ministry and witness of Indian church.

DW: In listening carefully to the deliberations and being in individual dialogues during the SSC meetings a number of issues for the future of Indian theological education within the Senate of Serampore framework came to my mind which I would just like to humbly submit and share with you and colleagues in the Senate as a way of continuing our dialogue. They come without any sense of prioritization or any clear expectations from my side and are just meant for not losing track of some of the conversations which were meaningful for me.

RT: I am happy that you have taken personal interest in the programmes and activities of SSC, and try to find some time to attend Senate meetings. Your interventions and suggestion are always very helpful.

DW: The new BD curriculum of SSC which now is in the phase of its implementation is a major achievement for the future of Indian theological education and beyond, as its principals, integrated, contextual and interdisciplinary approach are close to the priorities which were always seen as vital for PTE/ETE in WCC. As we have received several requests from other partners in theological education in the world to receive a copy of this document and overall outline it would be helpful to consider whether the key document for the BD curriculum could be either made available in electronic form to ETE to be put on the website here or – even more preferably – that the website of the Senate of Serampore is improved and updated to serve the communication needs with partners both within India and also with other partners around the world. There is a considerable need for more visibility of the work, the standards and new developments in Indian theological education to be shared with partners inside and outside India. A properly updated and renewed website of the Senate of Serampore could serve both cooperation between Indian theological colleges and also interaction with neighboring churches with less equipped institutions and networks of theological education.

RT: We are encouraged by your appreciation of new BD programme and curriculum. It was unfortunate that other associations in Asia could not be part of our deliberations and discussion in spite of our invitation. We are willing to share our experience and report with associations elsewhere and our Regulations and syllabuses will be available soon. I will send a copy of the booklet, Exercise in Curriculum Revision, 2006-09 for your reference. This is prepared for pedagogical institutes, and is being provided to all participants.

We are working on a new website (senateofseramporecollege.edu.in); we will need some funds to maintain it though. We are trying to generate the same.

DW: It might also be considered whether a regular electronic newsletter of the Senate of Serampore churches could help for the communication needs. Not everybody has the time and capacity to work and read through the complex printed materials distributed during the SSC annual meetings. For communication with partners inside and outside India (with partners in other parts of the world) it might be helpful to have an annual or biannual newsletter of SSC which focuses on highlights, key developments and new appointments within SSC colleges and thereby creating better communication and collaboration channels.

RT: We normally send annual Reports of the Senate and the BTESSC in the form of a booklet to our partners. It may be good idea if we can make it biannual and also increase its circulation. We do need additional information about those who are interested in our work. As you have suggested, the same can be posted in our website too.

DW: The video produced on the history of UTC is a remarkable start and good contribution for communicating Indian theological education for a wider audience. We would try to bring this into the network of Edinburgh 2010 preparatory processes to try to have this shown also during the Edinburgh 2010 centenary conference. As several Indian theological colleges have well equipped communication departments it might be explored whether there could be project like an all Indian video on the history of theological education related to Serampore College and the present system of Senate of Serampore College. If such a video would highlight key aspects and key contributions or unique features of some of the individual colleges it could serve as a means to strengthen the communication about Indian theological education, the fellowship with each other as well as communication with external partners. Sham P. Thomas expressed some interest in considering a project like this.

RT: Video presentation is a good idea. Some colleges, including Serampore, have done it. We are sure this can be further explored. TTS has prepared a very commendable video report of the convocation-2009 and the UTC also doing so. Its presentation on the centenary through video will help it to propagate the UTC and its concerns. Others may also follow.

DW: Some theological colleges in the Senate family have some direct partnership links with institutions of theological education in other parts of the world, however there does not seem to exist a survey of international partner relations or any general recommendation on policies and standards in developing international partnership links with institutions of theological education in other parts of the world. It might be considered whether it is appropriate to call together a Senate of Serampore committee on international partnerships in theological education as a way of developing, accompanying and strengthening international partnerships in theological education and evaluating positive and problematic experiences together.

RT: Your suggestion for international partnership link with institutions of theological education in other parts of the world should be taken for consideration. After strengthening the research department of the University, we can move in that direction with earnest. ETE may be requested to coordinate such a discussion on the part of those who are interested.

DW: The number of women representatives in BTESSC and SSC meetings at this occasion was comparatively low; also no representative of ATTWI was present (only ATTI was present). While there are probably complex and manifold reasons for this it might be worth considering whether some deliberate steps need to be taken to increase the number of women delegates to be sent by colleges to SSC meetings or whether other ways can be identified to encourage more women theologians to raise their voice in the common work or to organize themselves in a way. The historic achievements which are there in India with regard to women's participation in theology and theological education should be safeguarded and a development foreseen which does not move backwards.

RT: Participation of women in church polity has always been a matter of concern of the Senate. You have not, I am sure, missed the concern at this Senate too. We have asked the colleges to nominate women participants for BTESSC meetings next year. Unfortunately, ATTWI has its own problem, so also affiliated colleges. We are in the process of collecting list of women staff, and like to see if some more women are nominated in Senate and its Committees. Senate is much better as it has 3 members out of eighteen. We need not be coercive in our attitude but try to work with gentleness and understanding.

DW: SSC does have a continuous rise in the number of graduates in past years and legitimately is proud of registering the exact numbers of graduates each year. It is not clear however how and whether the rising numbers of graduates correspond to the needs of churches for candidates of ministry and their potential to offer job opportunities for graduates once they have finished. The question is whether there could be some long-term planning scenarios which would relate the emerging demands for candidates for ministry and ministerial training in member churches and the available capacities/places for ministerial formation/theological education in theological colleges (ratio between ministerial needs and capacities for theological training), as the situation seem to vary considerably between certain regions and churches and in some of them there seem to be oversupply of ministerial candidates whereas in other regions there seem to be shortage of trained ministers. Do churches formulate a clear scenario on how many ministers they need? Is there a long-term planning on how the capacities of theological education in India correspond to the envisaged growth (or diminishing) of some Indian churches? How are the changing profiles of young candidates entering for theological studies (less come from historical churches, more from charismatic and independent churches) reflected in a kind of a long-term scenario for the needs and capacities in theological education?

RT: Limiting the number of students in theological colleges may not be a good idea. We have colleges run by the churches, denominations and mission-oriented societies and individuals. The number can only be decided by colleges. Moreover, Serampore is only one of the many institutions engaged in theological education in this part of the continent. It is estimated, from unconfirmed sources though, that there are more than 2000 theological institutions operating in India. I have been collecting statistics through our new self-evaluation criteria Performa about graduates of colleges, where do they go after graduation; they are yet to be analyzed. We need further studies in this area before embarking upon some policy decision. Some of the colleges need to be encouraged to take up such kind of survey and do some empirical research. I agree with you that we need to look at this aspect too and embark upon some long term planning for theological education in this land.

DW: One of the roles of PTE/ETE has been to give grants for faculty development, important consultations and theological text book productions in Indian theological colleges as well as in partnering with SATHRI. Being aware of the need to avoid unintentional doubling of support grants for Indian PhD candidates and to provide clear transparence close cooperation will be maintained with SATHRI as to the continuation or phasing out of individual grants as well as a new overall strategy and division of labor which is in the process to be worked out with Asian partners in the area of grant giving for theological education as a whole.

RT: It is a good idea that we should work out a clear policy and direction for DTh scholarship. There are now seven centres for doctoral studies under Serampore; there may be a few additional ones in the near future. Research Committee may take up this matter and step-in to grant/allocate such scholarships to the candidates of the centres. There needs to be some kind of transparency in such awards as colleges may have their own scholarships for such studies.

DW: Several colleagues and Principals raised the concern for proper theological library development and more electronic resources for theological libraries. Vast needs are there and help and support provided by Theological Book Network at present does not seem to be enough and sufficient. While each college has its specific individual needs in this area the concern came up whether there could be something like an All India theological library/librarians association which could develop some common standards, identify common needs and develop a common major project plan for the enhancement and quality improvement of theological libraries in

India, including a major project for computerization (and common software program for all theological libraries). Otherwise it is left to each individual college to seek for its own partners and fragmentation will be emerging from this instead of common strategies for an all Indian national and regional theological library network (association).

RT: Library development is the major concern of the colleges and the Senate. Colleges need to be equipped with resource materials for theological education. It is also a fact that most of the colleges do not have financial resources for such a development. A comprehensive policy may have to work out to help the colleges, at the same time a few colleges in each region should be identified for developing their libraries as regional libraries whose resources should be made available to all affiliated colleges. E-library and inter connection of libraries is a good idea to begin with to tap the resources available elsewhere. We need to discuss the matter with colleges.

DW: There was a debate on dual affiliation of theological colleges and the need was emphasized to discourage dual affiliation in order not to devaluate the standards of the SSC system. While this is obvious from the perspective of the SSC system seen from the outside the question remains about the unity of the Christian church in theological education in India. Is there a need felt for more dialogue between the different accreditation systems for theological education which are at work in India and chances for mutual cooperation despite the fact that different accreditation systems cannot and should not be easily harmonized (ATA, SSC; Asian Pentecostal Association)? How to avoid mutual isolation and building up of negative stereotypes of one side over against the other? How best to serve the unity of the church in the future of Indian theological education?

RT: Dialogue with other systems of theological education should have to be taken seriously. Attempts in the past have not been so successful. It however does not mean that we should not continue to dialogue. We will surely take the matter up for discussion in Executive and see how the Senate can proceed in this direction.

DW: The status of the Senate of Serampore Colleges while being recognized within the Indian Serampore College (university) system still is not too clear legally in the international level concerning recognition of its degrees. Senate of Serampore Colleges (University) still does not appear on the international directory of universities and colleges (*http://www.4icu.org/*) which serve as a first source of information when western or African faculties and universities check the accreditation of Indian theological colleges. There is no mention at all of Senate of Serampore on the website of Calcutta university in the international directory (4icu) This lack of proper international registration severely limits the chances of Indian theological students to get admitted in post-graduate courses of theological research in universities and theological faculties outside India. What can be done to try again to get Serampore University properly registered in the University Grant Commission (UGC) and/ or Association of Indian Universities (AIU)?

RT: The matter of some kind of recognition of Serampore as a university by the government agencies needs to be pursued again. We did take the matter with the ICU who said that they will only mention it under University of Calcutta as they do not register theological/defense/religious universities. Serampore is empowered to grant degrees in theology only through the Serampore College Act-1918 of the West Bengal Legislative Council. We can act as a full university if we commence to grant degrees in other faculties too under Serampore College Act. But the Churches and government/international partners have not, so far, come forward to help the Council to go for it. Bi-centenary of the college in 2018 may be such an occasion to realize the full potential of the College and the dreams of the First and the Second founders too.

Please note that UGC has no power to grant university status to any university established by a law of the county. This is the ruling of the High Court of Delhi in 2008 and UGC had complied with it. Serampore is a university so established, and as such UGC has no say on this matter. We are trying to see that this status is clarified, if need be, we may approach the court.

DW: Some colleges affiliated to Serampore System have started innovative course and degree programmes with secular programmes of higher education in India (like MPhil programme in Mangalore). This is a promising development and seen from experiences in other world contexts of theological education there is a need to identify promising models of cooperation between church-related theological colleges and secular programmes of higher education also in other fields. It might be worth exploring whether programmes of cooperation between secular universities and theological colleges should be more encouraged as there might be a future need to also consider getting studies in Christianity recognized and introduced as part of Arts faculties in secular universities in India. The implications of increased expectations for common standards in secular higher education programmes from government ministries for education (for instance National Eligibility tests for doctoral candidates) might need to be seriously reflected. While keeping the needs for ministerial formation for candidates for church-related ministries as a priority, research on Christian tradition and faith could be regarded as part of national cultural heritage and a general knowledge realm of society which also should be presented in secular universities in the long run to allow for more interdisciplinary cooperation and public recognition of Christian values and tradition and to overcome dangers of an inward-looking niche-mentality in theological education and research.

RT: It is desirable that theological colleges have some understanding and cooperation with other educational institutions and universities. Serampore has very cordial relations with universities in Bengal. Unfortunately, theology department here has lost the prominence and innovation in recent years. Other affiliated colleges do not have such relationship except a few like TTS and KTC. We have been able to secure recognition for our MTh in some universities for doctoral studies. The research department of the university now should try to build up relationship and offer inter-faith and other research studies so that Serampore is not isolated. It is unfortunate that the Christian Study Departments, established by Catholic and Protestant churches in some universities, did not work out programmes for mutual interest; Serampore too failed in this direction. We need to take this up too.

DW: Knowing that several of these concerns will not have easy and short answers, but are related to complex fields and environments I just wanted to note some of the issues which I had taken note of to accompany our mutual dialogue.

RT: It was nice to listen to some of your wandering thoughts and response. We can work together in strengthening the vocation and privilege given to us in leading our people for His service.

DW: I am in deed very grateful for your open and generous response to the reflections raised. As you will have realized none of my questions were raised and meant in an attitude of knowing anything better, but just to humbly provide an external viewpoint and to take seriously the role of WCC-ETE to accompany the journey of one of our most important strategic partners, the Senate of Serampore College. I am moved by your way of answering in detail to each of the points and feel encouraged in our partnership of learning.

Chapter - 7

An Exploration of Indigenous Theological Framework

Wati Longchar

Introduction

This paper discusses primarily Asian realities and issues. The paper is divided into three sections: First, we will try to understand our common historical context; for understanding one's own context is the starting point of theology. Second, we will review some of the dominant theological frameworks and see how far they are relevant or irrelevant for indigenous people. We will analyze this from historical perspective. And finally, we will make an attempt to suggest a theological framework for indigenous theology exploring our own spiritual traditions.

I.   Indigenous Peoples in Today's World

Let me start with a story –

A group of indigenous theologians assembled in a consultation from 21-26 October, 2008 at Baguio, Philippines. When we arrived at Baguio city, we were informed that one of our indigenous brothers, James Balao was abducted for speaking for justice. Balao is an active researcher and trainer of Cordillera People's Alliance (CPA). He was engaged in research work of Oclupan clan and he was able to trace as far back as nine generations on two of the clan's family trees. This research gave them a sense of identity and solidarity among them. Balao's research feed into the work of the Cordillera People's Alliance campaigns against multi national companies to expose government misdoings and to assert the land and resources rights of the indigenous people. As a result of his research and active involvement in community organization, Balao was seen as a threat by Government. The family members and friends of Balao believed that his disappearance was perpetuated by the state. The CPA also believes that Balao has been targeted especially because of his vocal campaigns against the government's anti-people and anti-indigenous people's policies.

Some of us joined the International Solidarity Team in surfacing the abducted advocate of indigenous' rights, James Balao. We were surprised to discover that community were so afraid of the police and military because of the long history of Philippine leaders using the state security forces as a tool of repression which has bred deep mistrust amongst the population. In Lower Tomay this mistrust has been further compounded by suspicious faces in the community since the abduction, assumed to be plainclothes intelligence officers. It was shocking to see how real the fear of retaliation is within the community. We were even denied of meeting by Military Intelligence Group (MIG) even after prior information, which suggests an arrogance and a feeling of impunity which is unhealthy within the state security forces of a democratic country. After meeting several officials - PNP officials, Baguio City Councilors, Governor, Mayor, Commissioner of Human Rights Cordillera Adm. Region – we found that some of them were not willing to provide the facts, sometimes contradict each others and willfully ignore the fact in order to protect the state.

This is not an isolated incident. Global history of human rights abuse against indigenous peoples and indigenous people's activities has always been an element of corporate and government collusion. Such things are happening everywhere when indigenous peoples stand up for their individual and collective rights.

Whether they are in Australia, Taiwan, India, or United States, all indigenous peoples experience similar stories. We need to accept the fact that indigenous people are a defeated community all over the world. Their history is a history of defeat, suffering, and oppression. Their foreparents have suffered discrimination, genocide, exploitation and alienation in different stages of their history. The invasion began even earlier than European invasion in some countries, for example, the history of defeat of *dalit* and *adivasi* (tribals) begun in the hands of Aryan invaders almost 3500 years ago. In the course of history, the indigenous people became hewers of wood and drawers of water, and the nomads became kings and princes, masters and aristocrats.[1] In some contexts, it began with the wave of European contact, then the wave of western colonization, waves of western religion and education, wave of militarization, wave of constitutional democracies, wave of aid dependency and wave of economic globalization. They are a defeated people in all spheres of life. Today they are further marginalized through the processes of global capital regime.

The global empire and the greed of global capital are making tremendous impact on geo-politics of the world, and destroying and threatening all life, especially the poor and marginalized like the indigenous communities. In today's world, 'growth' is considered as the only principle for liberation. The concepts of 'care for one another', 'just economy' and '(sabbath) rest for creation' (Det. 25), are considered as non-productivity and the root of all human problems from poverty to sickness to political instability.

---

[1] James Massey, "Historical Roots" in *Indigenous People: Dalit*, (Delhi: ISPCK, no. date), p. 27.

Any attempt to slow down economic growth is labeled as immorality. The global market turns indigenous peoples and our cultural activities and earth's resources into commodities for profit. The weak, namely the migrant workers, farmers, consumers, small entrepreneurs and the whole eco-system are the victims of globalization. The barbaric atrocities, human rights violation, ethnic conflict, poverty, injustice, low self-esteemed, inferiority complex, alienation from earth-centred life and spirituality are all interconnected. Let me cite some examples:

1. Denial of Religious Rights: Many governments do not recognize indigenous people's religion as 'religion'. They are considered people without religion or sometimes they are clubbed together with a dominant religion. The Govt. thinks that to be recognized as religion it must have temple, mosque, cathedral, scripture, priest, saints, images of god or goddesses. Though indigenous people's religion is the oldest religion with distinct spirituality, it is still considered as the lowest form of religion and are not given due recognition. In some countries like India, indigenous people are being denied of propagating and professing one's faith. Majority group can involve in re-conversion, but minority cannot do it. In India, indigenous religion is still considered as upshot of Hinduism, though tribal people have distinct culture and religion. Conversion to Christianity is seen as threat and justified re-conversion.

2. Disappearance of language. A major function of language is to act as reservoir of people's identity and self-expression. It helps people to dream their dreams and assists them to articulate their hopes and visions of new future. Language is also one of the most important social agencies that create feelings of community by providing identity.[2] In the name of national integration, the

---

[2] M.P. Joseph, "Introduction: Searching Beyond Galilee" in *From Galilee to Tainan: Towards a Theology of Chhutpthau-thin* (ATESEA Occasional Paper No. 15) by Huang Poho (Tainan: ATESEA, no year), p. 6.

military junta does not allow to teach children in their ethnic languages in Myanmar. Children are being denied of learning, writing and speaking in their own mother tongue. Some indigenous communities have intentionally adopted the language of dominant community out of fear of discrimination. In Australia alone some 500 languages have been lost since European arrived on the continent. Even the names of the towns, cities, street names have been changed to Western names, especially to English names. The use of local languages was not only forcefully denied, but people were also led to believe that the use of and command of a local language exposed an inferior position in society. Can we expect survival of indigenous people's culture and value system without a language? With the lost of language, the indigenous people have lost their distinct social, cultural and spiritual values.

3. Denial of ancestral land: Most indigenous people have lost their land due to illegal legal system, development activities and political manipulation. Today land has been forcefully taken away from them and many people do not have land for cultivation. With the lost of land which is the main source of their livelihood and culture, they constitute now the biggest labour force today. Many of them are the illegal or unaccounted migrant workers in different countries, and they constitute the poorest section of the society.

4. Denial of Identity: Most of the indigenous people have been assimilated into dominant society in the name of national integration - Chinese culture in Taiwan, Hindu caste system in India, Burmese culture in Myanmar, Hinduism in Nepal, Islamic culture in Bangladesh, Indonesia, Malaysia, etc. Many indigenous people fear to disclose their identity. People fear of elimination when raise critical and constructive justice voice, particularly to speak about minority rights and justice. The people once with rich cultural tradition are now reduced to

"NO' people in many countries. They live in fear and uncertainty. Many people are now reduced to people with NO culture, spirituality, morality, identity and dignity.

5. In Thailand, Cambodia, Myanmar, Nepal, India, etc more than 40% of indigenous girls and women who migrate to cities, work in the sex trade. The majority of female trafficked across states borders in Asia are from indigenous communities. Being reduced to abject poverty, many of them have no option except to sell their bodies.

These are just a few examples. This is our common history and indigenous people continue to struggle with all these challenges. We are talking about people who are being crushed and denied of their land, culture, language and identity. We cannot do indigenous theology without addressing such individual and collective oppression, denial and abusive of power.

Theological Development: An Historical Overview

Do we address those issues in our theologizing? The history of Christianity among the indigenous peoples is between 150-250 years old. The Christian missionaries were the first people to come and work for the liberation of the people. They transformed the society by abolishing some of evil practices such as slavery, headhunting, lavish feasting, etc. Many modern institutions were first introduced by the church - the first school, the first hospital, the first translation work and the first printing press among many others. These all changed traditional societies. However, Christian missions, no matter which denomination or society, all considered themselves 'superior' and consistently maintained an exclusive attitude towards indigenous religion and cultures. They came with a strong view to conquer 'other world' by Christian faith. Conversion was understood in terms of replacement of the old ways of life which include rejection of traditional cultures and value system. Today many people have forgotten and uprooted from their traditional value system.

Roughly, we may divide the history of the development of Christian theology among indigenous people into three stages:

Receiving stage (1800-1950s): During this period, the churches were under Western missionaries. All the decision making, material and human resources for mission-work were controlled and came from the 'mother churches'. Churches were required to implement the policies or decisions that were made thousands of miles away. In their effort to contextualize theology, the missionaries pursued the 'Translation Method' of doing theology. Perceiving that the Western culture is superior and the only valid expression of Christian faith, they attempted to translate the theological formulations of the 'mother' churches abroad in appropriate native languages by means of adopting and adapting local terminologies, idioms and categories.[3] It was thought that Christian faith developed in the west is *the unchanging truth for all ages and for all contexts*, and should be accepted without any question. Therefore, native culture and traditions were never considered valuable resources for doing theology. Christians who participated in traditional festivals were excommunicated from the church. Drums, traditional songs, dances and value systems were condemned as evils and prohibited among the believers. There was very little or no awareness of the religio-cultural experience of the people. Theology was alien to the people; it spoke an alien language and ideas. Theology was outside of the people's reality. God's revelation was accepted in a very narrow way reducing indigenous people's religion and culture as mere *preparatio evangelii*. It was a period of receiving without any question. Theology was formulated elsewhere, imported from outside and taught by outsiders. The church and its theology was a stranger in the society.

Learning stage (1950s-1980): During the 1950s and 1960s, the national movement, post-independence reconstruction, nation-state

---

[3] OV Jathana, 'Indian Christian Theology: Methodological Reflection', *Bangalore Theological Forum*, XVIII(2-3), (1986): 71.

secular democracy, fight to end poverty, and development of infrastructures were some of the major concerns in Global South. The struggle for self-identity of the church, unity of the church and mission and indigenization or enculturation of theology became a priority for the churches. During this period many Western missionaries left or could not continue their mission work because of political reasons. This caused painful experiences of leadership transition within the church. The churches who were still struggling to stand on their own feet were left without trained leaders. However, the absence of Western missionaries created more space for local people to exercise their rights, responsibilities and leadership in the church. The legacies such as education, health care services were continued under the leadership of local leaders. The propagation of the Gospel among different communities or groups by their own initiative, the importance of promoting well being and social justice and safeguarding human rights are noteworthy as are three other theological developments or models of theology.

The *philosophical model* was borne out of the wake of nationalism, particularly during 1940s, in which many theologians in Global South became critical of missionary theology. They began to use freely the concepts, doctrines and symbols of other religions, especially Hinduism, Buddhism, etc in doing theology. They tried to work out theological hermeneutics in terms of Hindu/Buddhist philosophical thought pattern and thus, theological language became highly abstract and rationale. Unfortunately, like the other dominant theological reflections in the West, such theological approach became abstract and intellectual exercises unrelated to the real life situation of the people. It gave a notion among Christian thinkers that the indigenous people's spirituality is not philosophically deep enough to articulate theology. The indigenous peoples' view of life and spirituality were undermined and discarded in doing theology. People studied indigenous culture and beliefs simply from the traditional missiological perspective as a dark world to be conquered. People did not think or could not imagine that cultural values and spirituality of indigenous people can also enrich and help in understanding and contextualizing Christian faith in the cultural setting of the people. Such a one-sided theological paradigm again alienated indigenous people from their own religion and cultures.

In 1970s and 1980s the advocates of inter-faith theology made significant contribution with the employment of the *dialogical model* to do theology. A central theological claim of this model is that without taking into account the unacknowledged riches of God's work with the whole of humanity and other segments of God's creation, Christian theology cannot become authentic and liberative. Theology is seen as a product of creative and active engagement in dialogue with people of other living faiths and ideologies. Dialogical theology is to be celebrated for liberating God's revelation from the monopoly of Christians. Although the advocates of dialogical method were not always sympathetic and sensitive to indigenous people's spirituality, culture and religion, the affirmation of God's revelation and lordship over the world, in all cultures and religions widened the understanding of the mystery of God. In spite of the ambiguous nature of culture, God works in and through all religions and cultures. This understanding has created awareness to appreciate and respect the differences of others and also one's own spirituality, religion and cultures. Though some of the evangelicals are very critical of the dialogical method, arguing that it sacrifices the uniqueness of Christian faith, there is a growing awareness among younger scholars that we should go back to the roots to make Gospel rooted and meaningful.

Initially, liberation theology in Asia was greatly influenced and shaped by the Latin American liberation methodology. The indigenous communities, women and the other marginalized movements have widened the horizon of liberation theology from its Latin American impetus. Along with economic and political issues, the cultural and religious dimensions of discrimination are taken seriously in liberation theologies. It has influenced people to reread the Scripture from the perspective of the poor and oppressed in their struggle for justice and freedom. Commitment to the victims, the oppressed and struggling poor as the basis and the starting point of theology has inspired the alienated indigenous people to discover their identity, right and dignity. It has motivated people to engage themselves in new ways of doing theology by relating the Gospel to the socio-politico-cultural realities.

After the departure (even during missionary era in some churches) of missionaries, the three self-movement (self government, self supporting, and self propagation) in the church was launched by many churches. The contribution of Chinese churches is significant in this movement. Today we can proudly say that many churches are able to stand on their own feet in terms of support and mission. However, one important aspect was left out e.g. 'self-theologizing'. *Self-theologizing* was never considered as an important component for the self identity of the church until recently. This period of self-theologizing is now a dominant model of theological undertaking. In it scholars from the other regions/contexts can help to widen the theological perspective of a people. However, there is a difference between the *sympathetic* and *emphatic* theology. The indigenous people themselves must do their own theology relevant to their context. In other words, indigenous people themselves must take the healing of indigenous communities into their own hand. *We* must work for *our* own liberation and transformation. It was only in 1980s that many churches recognized the importance of 'self-theologizing' to make the church and its mission rooted in the actual life of the people.

The above mentioned theological paradigm is very limited. They are not capable of addressing the issues of indigenous people. We need to explore new ways do doing theology.

What kind of Theology Do We Need?

We need a people's centred theology, a theology centred on the vision of our Lord Jesus Christ. The past and present dominant theological discourses have supported and continue to support imperialism and anthropocentric orientation of biblical interpretation. Theological concepts developed in dominant theological discourses legitimized a religion for the one who is the master and the ruler and also sanction to exploit and manipulate all segments of God's creation for extraction of maximum profit. There is no place for the people and land who have been ruled and oppressed for centuries. We may cite three examples: (1) *The concept of God*. Theology is God-talk, a discourse on God. The discourse is based on a language which is symbolic and metaphorical. Metaphors are constructed out of a cultural or social environment and context. The dominant images of God developed in Christian traditions are images such as Ruler, Lord, Master and Warrior. They are all patriarchal, political and military images. These images have made Christianity a religion of, and for the ruler, elite and the upper-class. The theological concepts or images of God which we uphold today are in deep crisis because they are not capable of liberating the poor and marginalized people like indigenous people from unjust system and practice and unmindful destruction of God's creation. Such ruler's theology supported colonial governments, war, invasion and unprecedented exploitation of earth's resources. The world is now confronted with the fact that the imperil construct of the concept of God will not be able to liberate the people and nature who are the victims of power. (2) *The understanding of mission*. The discourse on God as ruler and master has reinforced a success oriented or triumphalistic mission. The languages like "Mission Crusade", "Mission Campaign", "Home Penetration", "Mass Evangelization" etc. are all military language and concepts. Christians, by and large, engaged in denominational expansion rather than God's mission. Success in mission is measured by how many churches have been planted, converted and baptized. Mission has been very exclusive and never recognized God's revelation in other religious traditions and cultures. Mission is God's mission. God is the owner of the mission, but not the churches. But Christians have manipulated and acted as if we are the owner of mission. (3) *The understanding of creation.* Dominant Christian interpretation of creation is anthropocentric – human is the reference point of all realities. Nature exists for human. Apart from rational beings, the other segments of God's creation cannot come under the scheme of salvation. There is no sacred and mystery in nature, but it can be manipulated and controlled for the benefit of human beings. To exploit nature is divine will. This one-sided theological interpretation again justifies expansion of colonial power and exploitation of nature. The ideology of globalization and the expansion of global capital market are deeply rooted on this interpretation. The unprecedented exploitation of nature and present ecological crisis testify the failure of the Christian understanding of creation.[4]

Discourse on indigenous theology can make a difference in our times by turning and rerouting to Jesus of Galilee movement. In Jesus' movement, we see a decisive reversal from empire and money to people in pain, from ruler to ruled, from oppressor to the oppressed, from individualism to cosmic vision of life. Jesus' movement was a people-centred and cosmic centre movement against the power of destruction and death. He stood for a different value system - peace, love, service and liberation of poor were the message of Jesus, but not the power, sword, military and mammon. Jesus became the voice of the oppressed and voiceless. Jesus' paradigm was people-centred theology. The option of, and for the "people in pain" as the locus of indigenous theology requires sacrifice and radical departure from the power, institution and mammon. We must reroute indigenous theologies in the context of people in pain and groaning of God's creation.

---

[4] I have already dealt extensively on this issue in my earlier writings. For more details refer to *Tribal Worldview and Ecology,* and *Traditional Tribal Worldview and Modernity.*

Indigenous Theology – Can we take Liberation Paradigm?

In the recent development of liberation theologies, we see a decisive paradigm shift in doing theology. For examples,

1. *The context: not the rich but the poor and marginalized* - The dominant theologies are considered as science of faith drawn from scripture and tradition. It takes the realities of the context of dominant groups and communities. The perspectives of the rulers and the elite become the paradigm for doing theology. Whereas in contextual theologies, the experience, hardship and spirituality of the poor and marginalized people like the indigenous people, women, the poor become the vital source for doing theology. It is a theology from 'below' and 'underside of history'. The marginalized and the abandoned people is the locus of the divine. The people are no longer treated as the *objects* but as *subjects* of history. We can apprehend God by what he has done and is doing for the people in the concrete historical context. The focus on the *ochlos* is the critical principle in contextual theologies.

2. *The sources: not philosophy, but people's stories* - In dominant theologies, the language, content and framework of theologizing are drawn from the philosophical insights and categories. A notion in dominant theologies is that theology must be rational, critical, logical and scientific in form and content. To do so, one must take the philosophical system and fit in the received theological concepts into that philosophical system. For example, we have a brilliant exposition of the existential philosophy by Bultmann, Tillich and the process philosophy by John Cobb. In this theologizing process, both God and the world are somewhat abstract concepts and, therefore, there was a serious failure to relate the Gospel to the concrete reality of brokenness, oppression and dehumanization. In short, theology became mere abstract and intellectual exercises unrelated to the real life situation of the people. However, in contextual

theologies, the sources are drawn from the experience of the people themselves. For Minjung theologians it is socio-biography of collective people's suffering in oppressive regime. Stories can also mean people's symbols, stories,[5] myths, songs, dances and other forms of expression become the source of doing theology. Contextual theologies draw more insights from other disciplines such as sociology, psychology, economic and other forms of reflective expression for the analysis and articulation of the experience of people.

3. *The Aim: Not defending faith, but liberation:* A major focus of the dominant theologies is to engage in systematic constructions of timeless theological concepts (they claims to be) beginning from the doctrine of God, the Christ, the Holy Spirit, the Holy Trinity, the problem of Evil, the Creation, Human, Sin, the Atonement, the Church and Ministry, the Sacraments, Salvation and Christian Hope. The primary objective of theologizing is to help people understand and interpret the God's act i.e. to give rational for their faith. Whereas the primary objective of theological reflection of contemporary contextual theologies is to help people in their struggle for transforming their situation

---

[5] Musa W. Dube writes that "stories and story-telling are central to African societies (it is same with indigenous people in Asia also). Stories are told and retold repeatedly to depict life, to transmit values and to give wisdom for survival in life. The art of telling and retelling stories remains central to African societies. For examples, a grandmother can tell the same story differently depending on her audience and the issues she wants to address. Thus characters in a story may change to suit the listeners and their circumstances, as the teller sees fit. A story may also be told to a group of listeners who add their comments and questions. This makes story-telling itself (and the story itself) a moment of community writing or interpretation of life, rather than an activity of the teller or author. The teller or writer thus does not own the story or have the last word, but rather the story is never finished; it is a page of the community's fresh and continuous reflection." See *Other Ways of Reading: African Women and the Bible (Atlanta/Geneva: Society of Biblical Literature/WCC, 2001), p. 3 ff.*

of injustice and oppression. Theologizing is a process that empowers people to transform their situation in accordance with the utopia or the vision of the gospel. In this sense, the aim of contextual theology is liberation. It aims to provide a vision for the future, and empower people to change the existing values and relationship. Liberation theology is integral to people's on-going search for their identity and struggles for justice.

4.   *Method*: *not theory but liberative praxis* - In dominant theologies, the pattern of theologizing as in many other disciplines has been, first to enunciate a theory (as in Biblical Systematic theology) and then apply it (Practical theology, Ethics, etc). The assumption in this procedure is that pure and true thought about reality can occur only when it is removed from act and practice; doing is an extension of knowing. However, in contextual theologies, liberative praxis is the method of doing theology. They make a distinction between theory and practice on the one hand, and praxis on the other. This is praxis-theology. It involves rigorous theoretical reflection, but it insists that it should emerge from the practice that is oriented to transformation.

What is the Distinctive Identity of Indigenous Theology?

As the indigenous people's theology is a contextual theology, a theology from 'below' and 'underside of history'. It aims to liberate them from their inferiority complex, from oppression and discrimination by attempting to rediscover the liberative motifs in their cultures and religion, and by reinterpreting the Bible and Christian traditions from the perspective of people. Hence, the focus and goal of the indigenous theology is liberation and transformation. It aims to restore their self-identity and dignity by creatively engaging on the Gospel and culture in their struggle for social, economic, religious, cultural, political and ecological justice. In the process of working for their own liberation and transformation, and creative participation in wider society, the indigenous people work for the liberation of both the oppressors and the oppressed.

It is, therefore, a theology that includes liberation of the whole humanity and of the entire God's creation.

Methodological speaking, the point of departure of the indigenous theology from the other contextual theologies is that, the indigenous theology seeks liberation from the perspective of 'land' because it is the land that sustains and nourishes people and give them an identity. Among the indigenous people, their history, culture, religion, spirituality and even the Sacred Power cannot be conceived without 'creation/land' or 'space'. The land and its inhabitants are two aspects of one reality. Human liberation will be void and empty without affirming the integrity of the goodness of land and its resources. Liberation without land is not liberation. It will lead to slavery and destruction. Therefore, the land and its resources that sustain and nourish all beings and give them an identity and selfhood is not merely a justice issue to be set alongside other justice concerns. It is the foundation of history, existence and identity.[6] Poverty, war, oppression, ethnic conflict and identity problems cannot be understood or solved without relating to integrity of creation/land. Justice to creation/land becomes very central to liberation and human dignity and fullness of life.

> When all the trees have been cut down,
> When all the animals have been hunted,
> When all the waters are polluted,
> When all the air is unsafe to breathe,
> Only then will you discover you cannot eat money.[7]

---

[6] For this insight, I owe a deep gratitude to Prof. George Tinker's article on 'American Indian & the Art of the Land' which appeared in *Voices From the Third World*, Vol. XIV/2 (1981) and 'Spirituality and Native American Personhood: Sovereignty & Solidarity' in K Abraham and B Mbuy (eds.), *Spirituality of the Third World* (Orbis Books, 1994), pp. 127-128.

[7] See Max Eidger, "Indigenous People – Spirituality and Peace", a concept paper presented at Asia Pacific Alliance of YMCAs and Interfaith Cooperation Forum, October 19-24, 2007.

That is why doing justice to 'land' is the starting point of the indigenous people's theology and their search for liberation. Commitment and dedication to the harmony of creation/land springs forth in love, nurture, care and acceptance. This methodological priority of justice to land is essential not only because of their 'earth-centred' worldview and tradition, but because of our contemporary ecological crisis, misuse of resources, market culture, war for oil and survival crisis of many people. This methodological priority of doing justice to totality of creation is the primary departure from the other contextual theologies.

Our Theological Perspective

No person or community can have monopoly over theology. To express our knowledge of God in one's own way is the inherent right of all human being. We can apprehend God by what he has done to our foreparents even before the arrival of Christianity and is doing for the people in the concrete historical context. Therefore, we are called to articulate our faith journey with God and community in our own way.

a.   *Biblical Testimony of Creation*

The indigenous peoples communities recognize several 'scriptures', including oral traditions to apprehend God. The Bible is the book of indigenous people. It speaks of people's relationship in society, cultivation, animals, nature and encounter with the Divine power in their search for liberation. The Hebrew Bible starts with creation of heaven and earth, and then moves on to creation account of humanity as created from the ground/land, that humanity is created in God's image and that each race and nation was assigned a space in God's world (Deut 32: 8). The land, from whose womb humanity was formed (Gen. 2:7), is also viewed by the Bible as really alive. It is not a mass of dead matter, but a living, pulsating organism. From our land-centered lenses, the mountains and hills and trees do sing and clap their hands. These are not mere metaphors or poetry. The land or the whole creation is alive, and it is so intimately weaved with the lives and struggles of the indigenous communities that the former groans in travail (Romans 8: 19, 22) whenever we, the people of the land, suffer displacement, alienation, exploitation, exile and persecution. The New Testament Gospel, too, proclaims how central the redemption of the margins is in the divine economy. Jesus always located his ministry within the farming or fishing context and worldview. Jesus' language, metaphors, symbols are drawn from day to day experience of the farmers, fisherfolks and their struggle for justice against the empire. In other words, the Judaeo-Christian gospel of the reign of God is affirmative of our indigenous worldview and spirituality that constructs our understanding of who we are and what we struggle for.

b.　*God in Creation*

Creation is the first act of God's revelation. God cannot be perceived without water, wind, trees, vegetations, sky, light, darkness, animals, human creatures. In this first God's act of revelation, God revealed himself/herself as *co-creator* with earth. The most striking aspect in this first act of God's revelation is "God is present in creation". The presence of God makes this earth sacred. That is why God entered into covenant relationship with all creatures. There are many stories, myths, parables, and even fairy tales of how the Sacred Power and the land sustain life together. This makes "the whole earth is full of God's glory" (Isa. 6:1-3). People always conceive of God-world very much attached to them in their every day life. Totem, taboos and other customary laws tied them together as one whole. To perceive God detached from creation/earth or mere transcendental being who controls life from above is not the biblical faith. We believe in God because God as the creator is present and continues to work with the land, river, sea to give life and hope. This affirmation is the foundation for life. The major problem in theology is faith articulation of human history without other earth's family.

c.   *Liberation and Integrity of Creation*

The Bible is the book that affirms life from destruction. The most striking one in the Bible is the institution of Sabbath and Jubilee. Jubilee, in the Biblical tradition, is an invitation to participate in the dreams and designs of the Divine to recreate relations among living beings through restoration and renewal of history. Jubilee epitomizes the hope for an eschatological possibility in historical terms, creating systems that are free from the possibilities of exploitation and oppression. Ancient seers introduced the concept of Jubilee through principles of economic, political and social justice within cosmic framework which inherently negates marginalization of any living beings. To actualize this vision, God revealed himself/herself as the liberator in Exodus event. More precisely, God is revealed as the God of liberation of the oppressed. "I am Yahweh your God, who has brought you out of the land of Egypt, out of the house of slavery." (Ex. 20:2; Deut. 5:6). Israel as a people came to know God as liberator through the exodus. By delivering the people of Israel from Egyptian bondage and inaugurating the covenant on the basis of that historical event, God is "revealed as the God of the oppressed, involved in their history, liberating them from human bondage." In exodus event, God took the side of the oppressed community; the people who have been denied the human dignity and earth's resources.

The Nazareth manifesto of Jesus reaffirmed liberation by proclaiming the Year of the Lord's favor. Jesus reiterated the importance of Jubilee tradition for liberation (Luke 4:18 ff.). The proclamation of the Year of the Lord is a message of liberty to those who have lost their land, personhood or status that they could return to their former position and ancestral land; both the rich and poor, master and servant, the empowered and the weak and even nature itself were all return to their original. The conflict with Satan and the powers of this world, the condemnation of the rich, the insistence that the kingdom of God is for the poor, and the location of his ministry among the poor for liberation threatened the oppressors which cost Jesus crucifixion. In the absence of a reorganization of life prescribed by the values of Jubilee, a just community is only an empty word. The spirituality of Jesus is martyrdom and that is why it is "costly discipleship". The resurrection conveys hope in God. That is why Jesus becomes the symbol of struggle for justice for indigenous people. To fight and resist against the new empire of global market, anti-people development activities of the present time is justified and it is the Divine mandate to participate in God's liberative act in history.

d. Our Ecclesial Vision

The church is a house of prayer for all nations, races and language. There is no barriers and discrimination in the house of God. The indigenous people, women and persons with disabilities are all invited to celebrate and share their gifts for common good.

We need to understand the household of God on the basis of the richness of God's creation. This is expressed in the plurality of his creation. Attempts to exclude others' form of expression are denial of God's richness. No culture, no community is excluded from this God's structure of creation. All are unique in their own ways and, therefore, no one has the right to dominate and suppress the other. Life is protected and it can grow to its fullness only by affirming of the beauty of diversity.

Indigenous peoples affirm a people-centred church, ecumenical unity but not a church of power, hierarchy, expansion, extension and conquest. What we envision is a church that respects, recognizes, affirm, support, promote, advocate for us in our struggle for self-identification and self-determination. We envision a church that goes deeper in the indigenous peoples experience, not only as object of study but especially as *subject* of ecclesiological and theological elaboration.

Chapter - 8

From Orissa with Love:
A Comment of Friendship in a World of Enmity

Siga Arles

It was in the early nineties in Oxford, England that first time I met Dhirendra Kumar Sahu. He was residing in Oxford and completing his Ph.D. studies. After completing my Ph.D. at the University of Aberdeen, I was still in the United Kingdom since my wife Nalini was working on her Ph.D. at the University of Edinburgh. I was visiting Oxford and I was told of the Indian scholars in residence. It was my privilege to visit Gnanavaram (present Principal of Tamil Nadu Theological Seminary), Idi Cheria Ninan (present Principal of the IPC Kottayam Seminary) and DK Sahu of Serampore College. It was a brief visit with "DK" (as later I learnt to address him), Manju and the two sons. Little did I realize at that time that I will soon be with them at Serampore College.

I.   Friendship and Hospitality...

January 1993, leaving my wife and two sons behind in Scotland, I arrived at Serampore College to take up the William Carey Mission

Studies Department as a Professor of Missiology. It was a Bicentenary project floated by the Serampore Council under the leadership of JTK Daniel. DK Sahu had completed his doctoral study and returned to his teaching position and I was delighted to be his colleague. We developed a friendship and his home was open with hospitality to me. We shared much in common in our theology and commitment. Both of us had two sons and no daughter! I have vivid memory of some of our experiences. DK and Manju were anxious parents. One night in February 1993, they put their two young sons on train from Howrah to Delhi. The boys were to travel to Mussoori where they were studying at the prestigious Woodstock School. Next day, as parents they hoped to hear from their sons. But there was no phone call. At that time we did not have proper phone facilities in Serampore. Cell phones were unheard of. Questions raced through the minds of parents. Did the boys reach Delhi alright? Did they make the connections? Did they reach Woodstock School? At every stage, the anxieties of the parents, particularly that of Manju, were visible. They kept going out to the nearest STD booth to phone. But the lines were not clear. They came back unsuccessful, unhappy, distressed and frustrated. I could empathize with them. To be out of one's own State and to be serving at Serampore with lack of good schools and facilities, was a sacrifice that every faculty member made to keep Serampore College alive. Often it was not appreciated enough by people who sat in leadership and on the Council and committees. Very quickly I learnt of the challenges of service at Serampore College. DK Sahu had already been there eleven years by then. He and his wife paid the price to serve at Serampore, which I grew to appreciate.

Within a short period DK Sahu, Ravi Tiwari, Alagodi and I were invited to be interviewed for the role of 'Vice Principal of Theology Department'. These men had been there over a decade and I was a new comer who had just arrived. Hence, I felt I did not qualify to be attending the interview. I did not want to appear as though in competition with my senior colleagues - that will right away spoil the prospects of good relationships. I told them that I will not go for the interview. Moreover, I suggested that the three of them should agree on a rota and send only one person to the interview and allow him to be the Vice Principal for a term or two. Then the second person could take his turn and allow the third one to follow. Ravi Tiwari already decided not to go as he already had been the Rector earlier. Alagodi withdrew and consequently DK Sahu alone went to the interview. The interviewing committee took time to interview but instead of appointing him, decided to call for more applications. Surely this meant pain and agony and hurt feelings for DK. The insensitivity of the interviewing committee shocked us. I raised questions with the Principal. "When we colleagues withdrew from competition and sent one person, he should have been appointed. To deny him the opportunity was to disgrace him before the whole community and to throw indignity upon him. Once humiliated how can a theologian function with confidence and dignity in a community?" I wish to register here the fact that DK Sahu had enough grace in him to accept this pain and to continue to serve. Few years later, he did become the Vice Principal and from that role moved forward to become a Bishop of the Church of North India in the Diocese of Eastern Himalaya. Later from there he rose to a national leadership role as the General Secretary of the National Council of Churches of India.

Pain was part of his experience at varied levels and situations. I remember DK's story of his father who was a faithful witness as a 'Barefoot Pastor' in Orissa. As a young son, often accompanying his father, a "barefoot pastor", DK experienced the rural life and its challenges, and often reflected upon them. When he was a student at Serampore College and now as a Professor, he knew the pains of poverty, the frustrations of rejection and the dilemma of being a 'nobody'. But because DK pulled through those experiences with determination, hard work and dreams - put in biblical categories: faith, courage and hope - God opened doors before him and led him further and higher. As a friend and colleague, I rejoiced in his strength to put up with, endure and await in hope for God's timing.

I recall another of our common experiences. Both our doctoral dissertations were published in the Peter Lang series "Studies in the Inter-Cultural History of Christianity" from Germany, my thesis in 1991[1] and DK's in 1994.[2] Both were released in Indian edition a decade later.[3] DK began to make contribution to theology and ministry widely with his articles in the *Indian Journal of Theology* and papers in various consultations.[4] At times he joked saying he wished he too was a missiologist! Then he too could fly around ...! My colleagues nick-named me the 'flying missiologist', since I flew back and forth between Bangalore and Calcutta and elsewhere. But soon, DK's hard work led him to positions which took him far and wide. His *Curriculum Vitae* reveals the grace of God that covered him and made him a worthy instrument of God from his Oriya roots to bishopric in the greater Himalayan hills and statesmanship in the wider church of the large nation of India.

Salaries for theological teachers were shamefully low. That too, in a campus such as Serampore College, where the Arts, Science and Commerce faculty were receiving their salaries from the government on UGC scale, the amount we of the Theology Department received appeared shrunken further and hurt deeply. Carefully we had to count the costs and deny many things to

---

[1] Siga Arles, *Theological Education for the Mission of the Church in India: 1947-1987 with special reference to Church of South India*, pp562.

[2] Dhirendra Kumar Sahu, *The Church in North India: A Historical and Systematic Theological Inquiry into an Ecumenical Ecclesiology*, 1994.

[3] The Indian edition of my thesis with an Epilogue covering developments from 1987 to 2005 was released titled *Missiological Education: An Indian Exploration*, Bangalore: Centre for Contemporary Christianity, 2006, pp540. The Indian edition of DK Sahu's thesis is titled *United and Uniting: A Story of the Church of North India*, Delhi: ISPCK, 2001, pp121.

[4] See the helpful compilation of DK Sahu's writings and his *curriculum vitae* in this volume.

ourselves and to our growing children. Frugality was not a virtue but an imposition. DK and Manju denied much to their sons - but yet took up care for the elderly in their native soil in Orissa. There was a sense of hospitality because of the cross and its allurement. Years later there were some revisions that paved way for some justice to theological teachers at Serampore. But DK moved off to be the bishop, the head of a diocese. But it sure was no fun to be in the hilly terrain of the Himalayas! Did prosperity follow the bishop? Perhaps not! He moved off to ecumenical work with the wider church.

The friendship and hospitality that I shared with DK and Manju was precious but short lived. Staying within a predominantly Bengali community of secularists, communists, agnostics and the majoritarian Hindus, we of the Theology Department were drawn for the whole nation – from Kerala, Tamil Nadu, Karnataka, Andhra Pradesh, Orissa, Bihar, West Bengal, Assam, Manipur, Nagaland, Mizoram, Myanmar and Bangladesh. We were aware the challenges of national integration, communal harmony and religio-cultural mutuality. Often we reflected on these themes from a contextual and theological stance. DK was a thinker who teamed with the rest to explore innovatively. Serampore College provided an ethos for such exploration while we put up with the many challenges of low salary, lack of dignity and modern facilities – and gave ourselves to the passion of training the young men and women for Christian ministry to which they felt called. Our partnership for the sake of the gospel built a bond of fellowship, a sort of fellowship of the suffering, which we took up on ourselves and worked tirelessly. As I reflect on my time at Serampore with DK, I remember with gratefulness the satisfaction that was mine in theological educational endeavour in such historic setting. I acknowledge the way DK and Manju stood firm taking the challenges and serving to fulfill their calling to teach. Soon they moved to Darjeeling and I moved back to Bangalore to join my wife who taught at the United Theological College. Though speaking for the rights of women in theological education, UTC had the strange paradox that it would not employ husband and wife together, even if the couple were qualified in fields in which the college needed faculty members. Hence, living at UTC, I took up the responsibility to direct the newly installed Consortium for Indian Missiological Education, a faculty development program in Missiology at Ph.D. level formed by 6 Indian colleges linked with the Asia Theological Association.

At various conferences and consultations, DK and I meet periodically and share our friendship. I render hospitality as each time I give him the latest book that I as a publisher released from the Centre for Contemporary Christianity. Now he is crossing over from the National Council of Churches to a new role in ministry. *As DK turns sixty, I am glad to present this essay in honour of him and to wish him God's best for the future. As he walks the narrow way with faith, courage and hope, it is my prayer that God will grant many more years of fruitful involvements in ministry to DK in old and new avenues and bring out much value for the growing of indigenous theology and ministry for our land.*

In this article I take two areas of concern for theological educators like DK Sahu and me – the need for the protection of the dignity of a theological educator and the urgency of the financial protection for a theological educator. Taking care of these two areas, we should be able to ensure the releasing of the theological educators for better dreams, innovation and initiatives in church and mission.

II. "Three Mile an Hour God" and the Dignity of a Theological Educator

It was Kosuke Koyama who wrote *Three Mile an Hour God*[5] after becoming popular with his *Water Buffalo Theology* and *No Handle on the Cross*.[6] His plea is for our theology to emerge from within our culture and world view. A fast mode God as depicted by the North

---

[5] London: SCM Press, 1979, pp. 146.
[6] London: SCM Press, 1974 & London; SCM Press, 1976.

American culture proves a misfit to Asia. Solomon Raj has identified this in his doctoral thesis[7] when he notes that the Lutheran theology and liturgy did not appeal to the native Telugu people to whom spirit and demon presence and their affects in terms of illnesses were real. Healing and miracles were a demand within the culture. Hence, many independent churches developed catering for cultural needs which Solomon Raj attests as the process of contextualization of the gospel. He positively relates the Bible Mission of Father Devadas as in the same vein as the Latin American Liberation Theology, Basic Ecclesial Communities and Contextualization. Similar is the evaluation of Subba Rao Movement by HL Richard.[8] Both of these case studies from Andhra Pradesh attest that the impulse for indigenous Christianity is at the root of the development of new initiatives in terms of independent church movements. They seek after contextually relevant modes of worship and lifestyle.

Asian Contextual Theology has grown through the second half of the twentieth century with the contributions of the many such as Takenaka Masao, Kosuke Koyama, Choan Sen Song, Kim Yong-Bok, Kim Chi-Ha, Aloysius Pieris, etc., S. Batumalai's *An Introduction to Asian Theology*,[9] John C. England's *Living Theology in Asia*,[10] and the *Asian Christian Theologies: A Research Guide to Authors, Movements, Sources* edited in three volumes[11] are few of the

---

[7] See P. Solomon Raj, *A Christian Folk Religion in India: A Study of the Small Church Movement in Andhra Pradesh with Special reference to the Bible Mission of Devadas*, (Frankfurt: Verlag Peter Lang Studies in the Inter Cultural History of Christianity) Bangalore: Centre for Contemporary Christianity, 2004 & 2009 reprint, pp. 332.

[8] See HL Richard, *Exploring the Depths of the Mystery of Christ: K Subba Rao's Eclectic Praxis of Hindu Discipleship to Jesus*, Bangalore: Centre for Contemporary Christianity, 2005 & 2009 reprint.

[9] Delhi: ISPCK, 1991, pp. 457.

[10] London: SCM Press, 1981, pp. 242.

[11] by John C England, Jose Kuttianimattathil, John Mansford Prior, Lily A. Quintos, David Suh Kwang-Sun and Janice Wickeri, Delhi: ISPCK, Claretian Publishers & Orbis Books, 2004, volume 3, pp. 768.

resource books for our reference on the history and development of Asian Theology.

For the Roman Catholic sector, a two-volume set titled *Theology from the Heart of Asia* represents the first comprehensive outline of Asian Catholic scholarship, including 27 dissertations, covering from 1985 to 2008, focused upon the Federation of Asian Bishops' Conferences (FABS). Published by Claretian Publications, these are reference books aimed not at general reading audience but scholars and others who understand the importance of the federation and its vision of church.

The contours of indigenous Indian theology have been shaped and reshaped by the many that were identified as the *Pioneers of Indigenous Theology in India* by Kaj Baago;[12] the second line of pioneers were added by Robin HS Boyd in his *Introduction to Indian Christian Theology*[13] and the elegant interpretation was made by MM Thomas of *The Acknowledged Christ of Indian Renaissance*[14] through the many national leaders such as Swami Vivekananda, Mohandas Karamchand Gandhi, Sarvapalli Radhakrishnan and others. The role of PD Devanandan, MM Thomas, Russell Chandran, Manilal Parekh and a host of others are acknowledged profusely. The lure of the challenge of contextual theology was heightened with the global input by Theological Education Fund in the sixties and seventies[15] and the whole of the post graduate study program of the Senate of Serampore College took new emphases in the eighties and nineties – we have scores of theses which explored into aspects of dalit liberation, tribal awakening and female emancipation as it related to the different people groups of India. Slow but steady, we

---

[12] Madras: Christian Literature Society, 1969.

[13] Madras: Christian Literature Society, 1969.

[14] London: SCM Press, 1969.

[15] See Christine Lienemann-Perrin, *Training for a Relevant Ministry: A Study of the Work of the Theological Education Fund*, Madras: CLS for PTE/WCC, 1981.

have an increase of the literature and impetus for constructive action to accomplish the mission of the church in India in relevant ways.

Theological educational process has been guided into constructive theologizing mode and the leaders of thought should be commended for their role. Despite our inner divide within the church with incessant linguistic communalism and regionalism, at times even caste entanglements, we have made progress in our compiling of what could now be seen as the rudiments, roots, branches and fruits of Indian Christian Theology. The Board of Theological Education and the Senate of Serampore College have contributed together as well as separately to the process and the particular contribution of SATHRI (South Asia Theological Research Institute) as the Doctoral program enhanced research studies and documentations which will provide strong roots for what is getting established as the tree of Indian Christian Theology.[16] All the theses written should be printed in book form and made available in a series to the next generation. Building upon these, the next generation of scholars ought to go further and much farther and identify the identity and mission of the church in India.

Theological educators are the ones who are to take the task seriously and think through the themes and instil inspiration and motivation in their students for creative work. In order for a theological educator to do this, he must be a dreamer, a visionary and a philosopher-theologian. Stanley Samartha spelt this out in his graduation address at the United Theological College in 1994.[17]

---

[16] Several of the theses written by scholars were published in book form either by SATHRI or by ISPCK or other publishers, which all are indicative of the developing indigenous theology and ministry. An example of this is MT Cherian, *Hindutva Agenda and Minority Rights: A Christian Response*, Bangalore: Centre for Contemporary Christianity, 2007, 2010 reprint.

[17] See Stanley Samartha, "The House of Intellect in a Field of Action", *Bangalore Theological Forum*, Vol.XXVI, No.2, June 1994.

The way he depicted the task and purpose of theologians and theological education were very meaningful. I commend his sermon to all as an insightful communication. He said,

> We live at a time when the world of *action* is regarded as more important than the world of *thought*. Deeds rather than ideas, context rather than content, relevance rather than depth, programmes of action rather than outlines for study, are given more importance. Intellectuals are marginalized in a society and theologians ignored by the church. The house of intellect has fallen into a state of disrepair and the field of action is enlarging its boundaries.[18]

Samartha did not call one to abandon the field of action but invited theologians to "spend some time in the meditative space of mind and spirit, where creative ideas germinate for the renewal of life" and suggested that "The credibility of the gospel has to be articulated in the house of intellect and its power manifested in the field of action".[19]

If a theological educator should think creatively and dream for a better world order and communicate such vision to students, then s/he should be a person with faith, character, courage, confidence and self dignity. A theological educational community in a college or seminary should provide the sort of ethos wherein the faculty members could develop these characteristic features, mutually inspiring each other to feel confident and to take up initiatives. But quite often the testimony from the many campuses of theological education appear detrimental in that they are filled with communal, linguistic, regional and factional tendencies which divide faculty members one from the other. At certain campuses, it is the North Vs South or the sons of the soil vs persons from other

---

[18] Quoted from Samartha's article cited above by Siga Arles, "Perspectives on Theological Education" in F. Hrangkhuma & Sebastian C.H. Kim (eds.), *The Church in India: Its Mission Tomorrow*, Delhi: CMS/ISPCK, 1999, p.200.

[19] *Ibid.*, p. 201.

States or one language group against another, and also one caste group in contrast to another. The loss of unity robs the faculty of the warmth of love and oneness of spirit, whereby instead of exemplifying the characteristics of the body of Christ, what is portrayed is carnal competition and corruption; instead of self crucifixion, there is a consistent crucifying of one another. The lack of positive modelling by the faculty then hinders the growth of the students into wholesome spirituality of the body life.

If such becomes the continuing reality for a year or two, the concepts of faith, hope, courage, dignity and creative theology take off and what remains is stale situation of a lifeless and dry spirituality, play acting, facades and unreality. Whenever invitations are received to present a paper or a lecture or a sermon, efforts are made to develop high sounding ideas and flamboyant content to impress the audience, but they lack authenticity and rootedness. A theologian who originally envisioned to radically transform the world with the application of the gospel, now mouths a lot of words, quotations and artificial articulations which lack the capacity to enflesh and enliven the dry bones! Involvements in bombastic and colourful events increase, but life does not flow in its abundance as promised by Jesus the Christ. Dry bones wane and wax around. Apathy and disillusionment hurt deep within underneath the appearances of spirituality and learning.

Thus a major problem of theological education is that the institutions of education allow for a wrong ethos to prevail. It affects the students with negative formation. Quite often the faculty members are divided and they divide the students. Often it is not the students who are the problem in an institution but the faculty members. I wish to identify the real issue as rooted in the dignity of the theological educators. When they are not affirmed with dignity by the board, the finance office and the administrative structure, faculty members naturally turn sour and become fertile grounds of problem. Let me illustrate!

Firstly, when the Governing Boards of colleges meet once in a year and the Executive meets few times, there ought to be a cordial atmosphere when they could visit with the faculty and staff in formal and informal settings. Fear on the part of the Principal that they may share their grievances often causes a secretive situation, wherein the faculty and staff are not allowed time to meet board members. Some board members try to pry in and find out information giving false hopes to individuals which is unwholesome. Many board members have no clue of anything that is happening in the institution and attend the board meeting without awareness and have no time to meet people or learn of the welfare of individuals. A very unrealistic situation exists where people govern without ground level awareness. They make decisions for people whom they neither know nor the contexts which they understand. Some such decisions and resolutions affect people and their families and ministries rather drastically. I remember a board meeting where one chronic spinster lady was arguing against the wage revision proposed for the grossly underpaid workers! She was well paid and had no clue of the struggles of an underpaid worker who could not feed his family properly and did not buy enough clothes or toys or utensils or basic comforts – and had no money to cater for the medical needs of his ailing parents. In another board meeting, the proposal that we provide transport to the children of our faculty and office staff for their schooling was denied by the board members who came from various parts of the country and did not fathom the local situation... there were no quality schools in the nearby township and parents desired to send their children to the good convents and schools in a neighbouring town which was sixteen kilometres away. This sort of ignoble administration by boards leaves theological teachers robbed of their dignity and self respect. It leaves them unduly in frustrations imposed on them by insensitive and irresponsible persons as board members. I am quite severe in the way I am depicting it because of my awareness of many boards and their behaviour of sinful and unacceptable pattern. This needs to be studied and necessary corrective measures ought to be undertaken without delay.

Secondly, when a teacher approaches the finance office to settle accounts and to receive reimbursements, the system ought to be shaped with respectability to protect the dignity of the theological educators. Often I heard of the hurts of colleagues whose bills are questioned and rejected and kept pending. Already under-paid and struggling to meet the demands of the family, they go through psychological trauma. Every question, rejection and delay makes them sensitive and they withdraw into seclusion. Some stop asking and suffer more and more emotional constraints and resort to spending from their pocket what money should have gone to the acute family needs. Studies on such realities will pave the way for correctives.

Thirdly, the faculty members lack supportive facilities. For instance, what secretarial assistance is available is reserved for top officers such as the Principal, Academic Dean, Registrar and Bursar. To computerize, format, correct and print the papers, minutes and reports, often the faculty members struggle on their own. Some times they rely on either their children or the students or commercial centres. They spend to get the job done and beg for reimbursements. I remember a faculty member who went on sabbatical to USA and taught in a college where he was provided with his own office, computer, telephone, secretarial assistance and treated with dignity. Upon return, he remarked with agony of the lack of facilities for faculty members in colleges in India. It is high time that we establish a dignified atmosphere of work for theological educators in order that they could feel confident to think of impacting the world with the gospel.

Persons such as Father Devadas and Subba Rao of whom Solomon Raj and HL Richard have made studies as to their creative explorations were independent of theological college and its control. Their creativity grew because of the freedom that they took for themselves. But the sad tale is that the educated theologians are dampened in their spirit and hindered by the ethos of our campuses from explorations and innovations. Urgent is the need for us to reflect on the campus realities in order to release the potential of our theologians for them to offer relevant theological leadership to the church in mission. Unless such freedom is ensured, there certainly is no hope for the right functioning of the theologians and no hope for correctives in the church and her mission. Towards the end of his life, MM Thomas was deeply concerned about the status of the church in India as without clear thought or concepts as to her role and mission in the nation. His anxiety was that the church ran its course without clear mind and there was no source of thought and mind to teach the church. "Who will give the mind to the church?" was the question with which he initiated to form thought clubs to offer 'the mind' to the church. Paul Siromani organized such a thought club in Calcutta in which I took active part during my time at Serampore College. Thomas did not particularly think of the theological colleges or theological teachers as the ones to help the church. There is a chasm between the colleges and the churches as often well acknowledged in consultations and seminars. Efforts to bridge this chasm were made at various points in time but they mostly end with talk sessions wherein the bishops and leaders narrate the problems and go through blame games but do not follow up with healing touch. After one such meeting at the CSI Synod I was amused at the narrow way one of the bishops was closed in his mind towards theologically trained lay persons in his diocese. He was in a city where there were many – almost about 30 colleges offering theological education at various levels, some at doctoral level too. Several did their external BD (later BCS) with Serampore and some their B.Th. or M.Div. or diplomas. Such graduates were well used by the pastors to preach and help with various aspects of the ministry in the many churches. But they were not ordained and hence could not involve in the sacramental ministry. I spoke to the bishop and told him that if he were to ordain these men and women –who are already heavily involved in the church's ministry- they could also help with sacramental duties and thus help the over worked pastors. The bishop categorically rejected the idea. His rigidity was born of a faulty ecclesiological perception and his keenness to wield power! He appears to have forgotten the heritage of the protestant tradition and the significance of the concept of priesthood of all believers. Instead progressing from reformation times we appear to now retrogress with the misconceptions in those set into roles of leadership such as this bishop whom I tried to interact with.

III. "Sound of Low Whisper", "Sound of Silence" and a New Definition of Courage!

DK has referred to the 'sound of low whisper' and the 'sound of silence'. He speaks these after narrating a story and ending it with a thought provoking statement: "Everybody is afraid. But the courageous person is one who is not afraid to be afraid". I agree with him that it will take time to register this definition of a courageous person in our perception. The statement appears paradoxical and nebulous. But it needs to be thought through! DK tends to attempt to be philosophical in his theologizing mode. I presume that it is not merely because of academic and scholarly concerns but also as a result of the frustrations suffered in the mismanaged contexts of service and life.

It is quite common that theological faculties develop inner divisions based on caste, language and region as we stated earlier. People who are made to fear and feel insecure begin to share common concerns and team up into 'the oppressed group' and soon suffer the oppressed psyche! Hatred towards those in power begins to grow and cause havoc in the faculty team. Either the hurt raise their voice and fight or they choose to suffer silently. Isolation and alienation become the common experience leading to the culture of silence or silent reaction.

In the many contexts that I described in which theological graduates, faculty members and theologians find themselves, they go through constant situations of 'fear' and its synonyms! At times it is the fear of losing a job, losing positions of leadership, losing incentives, it is the anxiety of not being able to meet needs, not matching demands, not getting opportunities and the frustration of the false claims of Christian community. Such fears are suffered in silence. They get shared amongst colleagues who share the same fate – but it is kept submerged with tight-lipped silence. Such bottled up hurts and fears and negative emotions leave psychosomatic illnesses among people who are expected to model Christian life and its values, including the gifts and fruits of the spirit. It will not be untrue to say that our theological educators appear sick and sickening, with lack of relationships and genuine fellowship. I had been shocked to hear tales about persons from their colleagues which vary from character assassination to professional molestation. How shall we promote healthy community life within theological faculties? Even though the number is low, within the few, there are divisions, competitions and incessant fights.

One area of the church's life where this 'sound of silence' is loud is the area of ecumenism. DK wrote his doctoral thesis on the formation of the Church of North India depicting it as an example of the growth of twentieth century ecumenism. He served the National Council of Churches of India for a term. Ecumenism did flourish in India and show much fruit to begin with. But the journey into ecumenism has gone through various stages. I wrote an article identifying how there was a 1) **Successful ecumenism** in the Church of South India and Church of North India; 2) **Limited ecumenism** as this only brought few of the major denominations together, leaving many others outside of the merger union; 3) **Stunted ecumenism** as there was no continuous process of bringing in many denominations into the union; 4) **Fake ecumenism** where "there are lots of verbal expressions and jargons which do not really pursue to accomplish the intent of ecumenism".[20] I think of the ecumenism that Roman Catholics exhibit as well as the carrying on of incessant talk sessions between CSI, CNI and Mar Thoma church as examples of this. "Signs of ecumenical relations are plenty. They remain weak and meagre compared to the largeness of the Church and the challenge of the context. At times forces such as the Hindutva movement have pushed us to stay together and stand together. This could be identified as 5) **Forced ecumenism**.[21]

> Certainly, we have come a long way. But my contention is that we have not come long enough or far enough into our relationships. Our concepts of superiority and inferiority do play their roles and even when we meet, we meet with invisible but energetic barriers. There is still much work pending in shattering our walls of separation. Ecumenism must come full circle to provide us a theological basis for unity – which we all assume we know it well; a practical basis for unity – which will demand structural changes; an economic basis for unity – which perhaps lies at the root of much of our dividedness; and a sociological basis for unity – which is what Hindutva is pushing us towards.[22]

DK concluded that the hope for the future is "The development of an ecumenical church transcending the boundaries of caste, race, regionalism or colour" which "would be the final triumph of unity in India".[23] May God fulfill this hope in the twenty first century.

As DK moves from his role as the General Secretary of the National Council of Churches of India, into a new future at the threshold of becoming a senior citizen at the ripe age of sixty, I am grateful that a volume of essays are put together to honour him and his service to the Church and Theological Education in India. From

---

[20] See Siga Arles, "Ecumenical Relations" in Joseph Mattam & Joseph Valiamangalam (eds.), *Building Solidarity: Challenge to Christian Mission,* FOIM XII, Delhi: ISPCK, 2008, pp. 223-231.

[21] *Ibid.,* p. 230.

[22] *Ibid.,* pp. 230-231.

[23] See DK Sahu, *United & Uniting: A Story of the Church of North India,* Delhi: ISPCK, 2001, p. 83.

all his experiences as hinted to above, rather than silence, we should expect a bold prophetic involvement of DK in the continued task of shaping contextual theology for the twenty first century. From his agony filled testimony of the Church in Orissa, a State where the unleashing of hate campaigns and physical assaults have inflicted untold misery for his fellow Christians at Kandhamal, there is urgent need for leadership to emerge to establish corrective process and healing touch to the wounded psyche. We hear the 'sound of silence' of the confused and hurt Christian community in Orissa. The sound has re-echoed in Gujarat and now it is growing loud in the State of Karnataka. Where next? The State Governments are either unable to contain or are unwilling to correct or are proving an ally to the powers that are inflicting persecution. The Centre has been beseeched to interfere in Karnataka. But it has remained silent for far too long. We cannot continue to keep the 'sound of silence'. There ought to arise a new theology of combat, a methodology of corrective compassion and a new missiology of invasive leadership.

Even as MM Thomas had asked "Who will give the mind to the Church?", today, there is a reiterating of the question that should be the theological task. How should the church in India unite together in **true ecumenism**? How should she conserve energy to address the Hindutva agenda? How should the missional task take new shape to infiltrate and influence the whole nation with the impulse of the Good news of Jesus Christ? How rigid ought the boundaries of the denominationalised church remain? What ought to be the emerging shape of the Church in India? How should the church break its 'sound of silence' and become the proclaimer of 'friendship and hospitality' with contextual impact upon the billion and more people? What shall be the way forward to take the people of the many faiths as allies in the midst of increasing godless materialism, narcissism, scientism and secularism?

Theologians like DK Sahu have their task cut out with the above questions. May God grant that DK should contribute to the unfolding of relevant theology with answers to these and other questions that our times shall pose to our commitment to the Gospel and Christian mission. At the Pre-Edinburgh Consultation in July 2009, there were brash voices proposing to replace the word 'mission' with the word 'witness' and to call for a 'moratorium on the use of the word mission' – they saw mission as a colonial word! DK was in agreement with me that we need a contextually relevant interpretation of our mission, a protecting of its essence and a promotion of its effect. Edinburgh 2010 has voiced the reiteration of the challenge of mission for our times. We shall look forward to an exciting future of working on the concept, content and convergence of mission in contemporary India.

Chapter - 9

A Leaders Toast - Leadership Tested

– Pratap C. Gine

Prologue

To propose a toast on celebrations like wedding, success in exams, promotion in work place, victory in election, etc. is a common scenario of the present time. This is mostly done to congratulate the successful persons and to wish the persons well for their future life and their course of actions. The centre of attraction remains the MC and more so the persons on whose success this toast is proposed. These successful personalities of the ceremony would only know how hard they had worked to come up to that stage. They would also know when they resumed responsibilities how their leadership skills were tested, even without their knowledge and perception.

Leaders and leadership issue had always been a hot topic in human history, particularly in the socio-political and religio-theological fields. What follows next in this article is a glimpse of what leadership is and/or should be, how leaders are to equip themselves for their leadership, what hurdles they anticipate in their leadership, and how to overcome these hurdles. This article, then, will conclude with a positive note or recommendations for the future leaders.

This article is dedicated to the Rt. Rev. Dr. Dhirendra Kumar Sahu, as he celebrates his 60th birthday with his diverse ecclesial, administrative and theological experiences. In and through this article I express all my good wishes for his life and ministry ahead of him.

Defining "Leader" and "Leadership"

There is no dearth of definition for "leader" and "leadership", and in whatever ways these two terms are defined, they never seem to become exhaustive definitions. Definitions of leader and leadership depend upon the context, setting, personal background, purpose of leadership, and so on. Any single definition on leader and leadership would become futile attempt to meet the need of all-round definition. Michael J. Quicke, therefore, enlisted a series of definitions on leadership from different authors and statesmen with different background and from different countries in the Appendix of his book.[1] All of these definitions are worth considering for the purpose of this paper, yet this would not be done, as in one way or the other some of these issues would come in the following discussion.

One definition, however, is worth mentioning where Walter C. Wright writes, "Leadership is a relationship – a relationship in which one person seeks to influence the thoughts, behaviour, beliefs or values of another person".[2] To be more precise, a person may be considered a "leader" when anyone or anything that leads people or the mass of objects towards a desired goal for the optimum benefit of the majority at least for a specific period of time, and the people and/or the mass of objects reciprocate this benefit in a proven

---

[1] Michael J. Quicke, *360; Degree Leadership – Preaching to Transform Congregation,* (Hyderabad: Authentic Books, 2006), 181–184.

[2] As quoted by M. J. Quicke from Walter C. Wright Jr. *Relational Leadership*: Carlisle: Paternoster, 2000), 2.

manner, is considered to be a "leader". This term, however, at times may seem to be a relative term, as there may be a tendency to redefine it for one's personal gain.

Considering the etymological background of the word "leader" and its terminological expressions, one may tend to describe it as "ruler", "authority" and even "judge". In such cases, the term "leader" would indicate a person who is capable to lead with authority, love his/her people without discrimination, and on whom people depend with a positive direction for common good and gain. Any deviation from this "common good and gain" can lead to nepotism, corruption, and aberration.

Whether the public/followers of the leader spell it out or not, there is always an expectation of minimum *standard* from the public what their leader should be and what would be the outcome of his/her leadership. Deprivation of any sort is retorted in different ways, and a capable leader reads it well before the unruly behaviour goes out of hand. An apt leader would impromptu take necessary steps for rectification. Any act of retribution leads to confusion and creates enmity between the leader and the led. Naturally, then, question is what do normal people expect from a leader and how can a leader reciprocate their expectation.

Expectation from a Leader
1. Although leaders are considered as "born and not made", their leadership need to be affirmed within themselves in one hand, while on the other, by their close associates or followers. If this is not so, then a leader is bound to falter.

2. Leaders must have the quality to formulate message, communicate to others, be prepared to have feed back, listen to people's desire (if not demand), willingness to be part of the common people, and to have an aptitude to dwell on the ground. Alienating from the common people in thought and deeds is sure to produce counter result.

3. Leaders must be above any bias and discrimination. They must be persons with integrity. Their words and deeds must go hand-in-hand. In other words, leaders must walk the talk.

4. A leader should have willingness to learn from others and from adverse situations. Although a leader is expected to be an *expert* in every field and a supplier of advice for all problems, in reality it does not happen. His/her willingness to learn from others, and more so from their own followers, exhibit their positive qualities, which in turn can transform their foes into friends. Adamant nature of not accepting limitation of knowledge and experience is detrimental to good leadership.

5. The demand for a good leader had never been as high as we have today. Today the church is looking for a leader who would, in one hand, be Biblical faith-oriented, courageous, culturally alert and proactively visionary men and women, while on the other, he/she would be "impassioned scholars" who would wrestle with the modern questions and deal with their thought-provoking writings.[3] Personal qualities, accessibility to others, desire to learn continually and equip educationally can become great assets for aspiring leaders.

6. A leader must keep his/her people informed with latest information available, and make it a point that this is communicated to the targeted community. This can produce a participatory community.

7. Telling the truth is a great virtue for an aspiring leader. The leader must tell the truth at all cost. This will make the leader trustworthy and the people cooperative.

---

[3] Steve Hobson, "Creative leadership development: Breaking out of the traditional seminary mold", in Manfred Waldemar Kohl & A N Lal Senanayake (Eds), *Educating for tomorrow: Theological leadership for the Asian context*. New Expanded Edition (Bangalore: SAICS Press, 2007), 3-28.

8. It is expected that a leader acknowledges his/her mistakes in case he/she has committed something wrong either by commission or by omission. Admitting one's mistake is a great virtue which restores the person's credibility. Asking pardon from the subordinates would certainly elevate the leader's image in the mind of their people. Acknowledging one's mistake and asking apology for the mistake would necessarily help the leader to amend his/her future course of action and behaviour.

9. Acknowledging qualities or gifts/talents of the subordinates and declaring it publicly displays good gesture of a leader. A simple pat for the work done and a word of appreciation can do wonders.

10. Identifying the most important issue faced by the people and dealing with it decisively is a rare quality that people want to see within their leader. The ability to detect the crisis-factor and isolating it for common good with a provision for rectification is a quality that would grow side by side with a good leadership quality.

11. Dealing with people at par and not indulging in the act of character assassination is a great virtue that every leader needs to cultivate. Every attempt to maintain the *sanctity* of the community is praiseworthy act of a leader.

12. Spirituality of a leader is a great asset which can do good both for him/her and the people. Leader's spirituality brings blessings to the community, whereas unrighteous act of the leader brings disaster. In an era when commercial ads motivate people for good or bad, slackness in disciplining one's life can mar the life altogether. Falling into the trap of immoral practices is quite possible unless appropriate precautionary measures are taken.

Factors that influence leadership to grow

Depending on the situations leaders are either chosen or elected, and the chosen/elected leaders are to perform their duties in order to prove their worth. Likewise the leaders also expect some congenial atmosphere where they can play their leadership role. Once this mutual understanding takes place leaders can grow with their leadership skill.

Secondly, either the appointed body or the appointed person has to set the goal for the organization to function. Once the goal is set the leaders would then execute their plan, and they won't find it difficult to proceed towards that goal.[4]

Thirdly, the initiation of *ownership of stakeholders* can create a new culture of ownership and thereby a spirit of work culture can be introduced. This would, in one hand, encourage the leader to work, while on the other hand it will create provision for testing the leader's leadership role. Leaders are tested when stakeholders play their creative roles.[5]

Fourthly, a leader would require an atmosphere of coaching and being coached. A true spirit of coaching and being coached, transformation and being transformed and leading and being led would make the leadership to flourish. What Mother Teresa did through her Missionaries of Charity is nothing but a *movement* through which the common people were inducted to leadership that transcended all age-old understanding of leadership.

Tests of Leadership

There is dearth of good leaders in our society today. It is an irony that many leaders come to the positions of leadership in churches,

---

[4] Manfred Waldemar Kohl, "Theological education: What needs to be changed?", in Manfred Waldemar Kohl & A N Lal Senanayake (Eds), *Educating for tomorrow: Theological leadership for the Asian context*. New Expanded Edition (Bangalore: SAICS Press, 2007), 29-55.

[5] John Baldoni, *Great communication secrets of great leaders*. Tata McGraw-Hill Edition. (New Delhi: Tata McGraw-Hill Publishing Company Limited, 2004), 8-9.

Christian institutions, and even in theological colleges and seminaries with little or no training in leadership and management. They neither know how to handle with their responsibility nor are they willing to go for training of leadership. Sometimes the little good they do can be destroyed by the precautions they fail to take. Thus both they and their organization/institution sink together gradually. In fact, the role of leadership is dangerous. It is risky as well. The history of the world records the lives of great and terrible leaders and what they accomplished through others. There are leaders who on the one hand moved men, women, and mountains for tremendous good, but at the same time, there are leaders who hold the power and have done irreparable damage to the human society.[6]

Leaders and their leadership are tested at every step of their lives. If the leaders know this simple fact it is good for them. If they do not know, a little precaution can serve a good purpose. Below is given a summary of the areas through which the leaders are tested:

1. The act of receiving the mantle: The leaders get overwhelmed after receiving the mantle but without realising how much people have put their trust on them. This trust is entrusted to the leaders with a hope that they would *deliver the goods* in the stipulated period of time. Most of the leaders fail to perceive this unwritten test.

2. Abhorrence of arrogance: The *honeymoon period of leadership* ends without the knowledge of the leaders when they encounter severe criticism in different meetings. Any General Meeting or meeting of the Executives make them aware that people do not promote or support any dictatorial arrogance. People test any sign of arrogance within their leader, and if they found they abhor.

---

[6] Hans Finzel, *The top ten mistakes leaders make* (Secunderabad: CCMI & OM Books, 2004), 12.

3. Sincerity not at the cost of people: Sincere leaders are ought to become people-oriented in their every action. But this does not happen always. The leaders tend to become work-oriented rather than people-oriented. They fail to establish relationship with the people who brought them to this stage of leadership. Such behaviour alienates them from the people. As a result their leadership becomes subject to people's test.

4. Test on collegiality: All leaders know it well that without the cooperation of their subordinates they can never attain success, yet the number is so minimum of those leaders who acknowledge the contribution of the subordinates and maintain collegiality with them. The subordinates keep vigilant eyes on their leaders and test their collegiality.

5. Test of integrity: The careless and inapt leaders have to time and again face the test of integrity. The practice of nepotism, dictatorial attitude, ignorance about the well-being of the subordinates, indifferent attitude towards the general public, and the like are the result of the lack of integrity. The public in general and the subordinates in specific test the integrity of their leaders through different means.

This list is not exhaustive. There are many ways through which leadership is tested. It is necessary, therefore, to find out the ways and means to withstand these tests.

Ways and Means to Toast Leadership

Leaders are human-nominated but divine-ordained. Although they are tested at different stages of their leadership, their genuine service to humanity and honest dependency on God deliver them from falling. Mentioned below a few notes on toast of leadership:

1. Attitude of Servitude

To make oneself humble is a difficult job, yet it is so much desirable, if a person wanted to become a leader. This is a biblical teaching.

Humbleness pays both now and in the future. This provides opportunities to rejoice with the subordinates.

2. *Ignore Gossip, Go Ahead Instead*

To counteract criticism is a virtue but not with arrogance. Accepting blame may be a virtue but not blaming others. By counteracting criticism with positive attitude, leaders can reaffirm their integrity. Accepting blame may prove leaders' humility and shut up critics' audacity. But blaming others is a cowardly act. Blaming is a system of avoiding responsibility. The leaders should not have any excuse for their failures and they cannot escape from their mistakes. Likewise, leaders should not attempt to rationalize their act when they have made mistakes. Rationalization is a mental technique which allows the leaders to be unfair to others without feeling guilty.[7]

3. *Dare to do Things Together*

Leaders' down-to-earth attitude and daring to do things together can produce great result. This makes the leaders not only accessible to their subordinates, but also the subordinates feel at ease to assist their leaders. In turn, instead of ruler-ruled relationship they develop a relationship among partners.

4. *Respect Diversity*

Diversity is the gift of God. In respecting diversity one respects God. God is to be found in diversity of gifts, colour, creed, sexual orientation, design, views, look, language, and in anything and everything. Behind each entity there is a great purpose of God. All are "good" in the sight of God. Nothing can be ignored. When leaders are deeply rooted in this philosophy of life and the design of God, they would surely enjoy their leadership, and the people under their leadership would enjoy their life together.

---

[7] M. Chandrakumar, *Leadership Insights from Heroes of the Bible* (Secunderababd: Authentic Books, 2009), 299-300.

5. *Centrality of Christ*

Leaders' dependence on Christ and Christ-experience becomes the foundation stone of their success.[8] No adverse situation can have any spell upon them. All leaders need to be rejuvenated by the Spirit of the Lord in their leadership role; failing to which their lives would become boring and unsuccessful.

Conclusion

To become a leader is not a cup of tea for everyone. A prospective and aspiring leader has to go through different ups and downs, pass through different tests, and then only one becomes a leader. There would always be people for the leaders to propose toast, and there will also be people for the same leaders to test their leadership role. To conclude with the words of M. Chandrakumar, readers can win over their tests when their focus moves from:

> "Success to Significance, Fancy to Faithfulness, Believing to Following, Silence to Speech
>
> Weeping to Singing, Ignorance to Discovery, Guilt to Responsibility, Despair to Hope
>
> Individualism to Partnership, Conformity to Courage, Dominion to Servanthood
>
> Peace keeper to Peace maker, Good Friday to Easter".[9]
>
> May God continue to bless the Rt. Rev. Dr. Dhirendra Kumar Sahu in all his undertakings!

---

8 Michael J. Quicke, *360;Degree Leadership – Preaching to Transform Congregation*, (Secunderababd: Authentic Books, 2006), 59.

9 M. Chandrakumar, *Leadership Insights from Heroes of the Bible*, 305–306.

Chapter - 10

'Silence' : The Sound of Poverty
Bibhudutta Sahu

The Life of Silence

Standing on the third floor of the air-conditioned confines of the Crown Plaza, overlooking the city of Bhubaneswar on a crisp mid-March morning, the stark contrast was hard to miss. We had gathered for a strategic alliance of NGO representatives to discuss the roadmap of development. The Crown Plaza is located just off the national highway No.5, surrounded by residential complexes. After you have passed the iron gates, a turbaned concierge welcomes you with a deep voice that jolts you out of your reverie from the tranquil surroundings. From the 2nd floor, the high trees on the perimeter conceal the very world that stands in stark contrast to the one that I am experiencing now. As our air- conditioned cars cross the iron gates and turn at the corner to join the main road, you can't help but notice a group (microscopic representation of millions of Indians) of 50-60 daily labourers, under the scorching sun carrying their tools of masonry for that one chance that will satisfy their need for today- Work. While we were animatedly engaged in conversation about the plight of the poor in Orissa, they stood or squatted on the pavements in silence with their heads hanging low

in rapidly dimming hopes of employment for the day. Poverty has
a sound-Silence.

Contextual Reality

That silence rooted in poverty is the most disturbing indication of
the injustice that is being suffered by millions around the world.
While we casually use the term 'culture of silence', we cannot
understand the debilitating effect that it has had on the psyche of
the poor. This repressed silence has been witness to the grossest
forms of denial of rights and exploitation of the dalits, adivasis,
religious groups, women and children over the centuries. Every
imaginable step is being taken to take away what remaining
resources or knowledge they have been custodians to. This silence
is borne out of the relationship that designates one as the receiver
and the other as the giver. It is a norm that cannot be broken without
consequences. From the day that the child is born, he is conditioned
to obey power in the form of positions, age, physical strength, wealth,
and the masses. There is the additional burden for the girl child as
she has to deal with the compounding forms of gender
discrimination. Since time immemorial, there is in place an economic,
political, religious and cultural structure that has continued to
oppress the poor into silence. Any retaliation by the individual to
break the culture of silence has resulted in fatal retaliations like the
cold blooded massacre of the Dalit family Bhotmanges[1] in
Maharashtra, the attacks on various forms of livelihood of the dalits
in Kolhapur as they aspire for better sources of incomes in better
locations. The cold state supported killings of 9 adivasis in
Kalinganagar as they struggle to retain their control over their land
and the resources in an indication of the leanings of the government.

---

[1] The Bhotmange incident refers to the killing of all the 5 members
of the Bhotmange family in Khairlanji, who are dalits due to the
demands of the upper caste to construct a road through their fields.
The Bhotmanges opposed the plan. In retaliation, the women were
raped and killed.

The poor are continuously expected to observe the rules and norms handed down the ages as they are deprived of their right to decide their course of action.

The power of silence cannot be explained but needs to be experienced firsthand. During one of many informal interviews conducted in the organization, I came across a young adivasi man who is a supervisor in the tea gardens in Assam, India. It was a routine interview with the exchange of introductions, expectations and development understandings. This was to continue for an hour and we were heading nowhere with this interview. There was an admission that he was not aware of the terms or the work of the organization and deemed himself unfit for this organization. And then there was a silence that gave way to an evening of such emotion that we were swept away into the world that he had seen, heard and felt. He narrated his story from his childhood, his family's life in the tea-garden, the exploitation of the tea-garden community, his father's expulsion, his mothers' additional burden of providing for the family, his struggle to acquire an education, his rise to the post of a manager and the subsequent exploitation that he had to inflict on his mother as part of the management policy. His narration transported us to his world and exposed so vividly the realities of being an adivasi, effects of globalization, his internal struggles, denial of rights, divide-and-rule policies of managements and total suppression of resistance. For the next hour or so, as we listened, we were silent. This interaction reminded me of the prophet Jeremiah wherein he confesses his inability to speak as he was just a youth. The God we believe in chooses the most unlikely of moments and persons to speak to us and the impression remains with you for a lifetime.

Dichotomy of Development

The silence of the poor is further deepened through the various Development projects undertaken by the government. Behind the facade of development lie the interests of a few individuals riding on the pain and total violation of human rights of the poor. Development has become a much maligned word due to our attraction to look at the world through the same lenses called the neo-liberal economic model. This model propagates the principle of profit over people at any cost with people seen as simply a means to an end. It further promotes a lifestyle that believes in fulfilling the needs of today without thinking about tomorrow. The lack of long term vision towards the use of resources is endangering our very existence. A majority of the citizens marvel at the development of industries, dams, nuclear plants and term it as a positive trend. Such a skewed view is affecting the lives of 70% of the villages as the promise of development comes at the sacrifice of their lives, property and identity. In order to fulfill our greed, the poor must sacrifice their needs.[2] And still we expect the poor to stay silent. Now that is not the belief that we, as Christ-ians should subscribe to. Development has to be seen from the perspective of the majority of the poor and marginalized. Not only that but it should be visible that development benefits them.

There are a plethora of policies ranging from the NREGA, Forest Dwellers Act, Orissa Land reforms act and Chotanagpur Tenancy Act but we are still witness to the violation of the Act and policies. In the instance of organic farming, food crops production and public transport, we can see very clearly that these initiatives have policies that encourage the opposite. The subsidies provided for imported seeds, cars, and chemical fertilizers is acting as deterrent for the citizens to make the transition from unsustainable development to sustainable development. The lack of support for the cooperatives for those engaged in collecting forest produce. It is evident that the government is shirking its responsibilities towards for the local entrepreneurs in favour of the MNC's. The lack of support for the providing market support is proving a hindrance for the local entrepreneurs. In fact in many of the cases in Orissa,

---

[2] Current land struggle in POSCO.

it is apparent that these policies can be used for the benefit of the communities.

It is ironic that the government resorts to the use of arms, force and violation of all human rights granted within the constitution but cries foul when the communities join hands in revolt and attack them back. How many of us in our sound minds would allow the government to just walk into our houses and take all our houses and incomes despite having complied with all legal obligations? None I would hope! And therein lies the key to breaking the culture of silence. I do not support the use of violence as a means to an end. But it is also important to note that the government has become adept in applying violence as a strategy to terrorize people as they are sure that the communities will not respond with violence. There lies within us a point of no return: beyond which no compromises can be made.

False Alternatives

The prices of food have shot up through the roof. The rationale is provided that such a rise is necessary since the price of oil has also been rising. There is another explanation that such a price hike won't affect many since we have also revised the 6th Pay Commission. Both of these explanations tend to fall flat on their faces as we are looking at this problem from the wrong perspective. We need to de-link the price of oil from the rising food prices. It is only because we are shifting from a largely self-reliant agricultural nation to one that is becoming dependant on imports. They key lies in viewing the growth of the agricultural sector from one of a liability to that of a life-blood of India. We would need to explore further the possibility of local production to local consumption, crop diversification within the same district or block. That would in turn reduce the dependence on oil to a large extent. And yes, there has been euphoria over the implementation of the 6th Pay Commission. But unfortunately someone forgot to point out that there are over 700 million people for whom the 6th Pay Commission holds no relevance. But they would have to continue to bear the indignity of further reducing the quantity and quality of the food that they consume. Poverty hits where it hurts – Our right to food and existence.

As is it with us, the house (land) is our life, identity, sense of support and an emotional link. Everyone was witness to one of the ugliest family legal battles of the Ambanis over access and control of the Reliance Industries. The adivasis of Nayamgiri, Kandhmal, Kalinganagar, Khunti are also fighting for their land and right to life. These two examples need to be placed into perspective: firstly, the former is a struggle for greed and the latter is a struggle for basic needs. Secondly the dichotomy in the scale of the struggle is clearly visible with the brothers fighting an expensive legal battle while the poor have barely enough money to approach the courts. Thirdly, there has to be something distinctly erroneous when 300 million of our countrymen are fighting for their basic survival.

The survival of the poor depends on the **access, availability and affordability** to the various resources. The most common of these resources would be land, water, plants and animals. Now if we were to change our lenses and are forced to ask the question: to what extent are the resources available for the poor and marginalized, does the adivasi have access to the resources and is it affordable? The relationship of '**Jal, Jangal and Jameen**' extends far beyond the physical and economic attachment and enters into a spiritual, emotional and identity enhancing realms that we are not accustomed to or have not experienced. We can definitely try to empathize but cannot fathom the extent of the bond that nature has on the adivasis. In the instance of the forest dweller, there are two scenarios that could unfold: a) the resources are available but he has no access to them and b) the resources are depleting with the gradual decline in forest cover and hence the irrelevance of the question of access. Wherein in the resources are available and access are both attainable, the question of affordability in terms of marketing, product preparation, market access and input costs. The critical question is whether they are able to make the transition? Therefore the response to this question takes on political dimensions.

Silence as Realization

Silence is nothing else but the sign of something powerful to come. Silence in a person for a prolonged period of time is an indicator that there is a volatile package of emotions waiting to erupt. Now just multiply that by 300 million repressed emotional packages just waiting to burst out. The right to ensure a life of dignity cannot be condoned any longer and needs a response that will break the culture of silence. The rise of social movements provides us with the answer that proposes that the political and economic spheres remain the fundamental points of control that need to be occupied. The pivotal point for the mobilization of the people lies in the commonalities of the injustices faced and experienced.[3] The social movements provide the oppressed a platform from which to exert their power to realize the change that they have been visualizing. Social movements have proven to be successful as they are inclusive in nature, are optional and yet provide the individual to be an active decision maker / actor. Charles Tilly[4] observed that social movements draw their strength from Worthiness, Unity, Numbers and Commitment. Throughout the centuries, the oppressed have been made to feel worthless by socio-politico-cultural structures and have been divided on grounds of class, caste and gender. It is widely recognized that their strength lies in the numbers that they

---

[3] Sidney Tarrow defines [Tarrow, 1994] a social movement as *collective challenges [to elites, authorities, other groups or cultural codes] by people with common purposes and solidarity in sustained interactions with elites, opponents and authorities.*

[4] Charles Tilly defines big social movements as a series of contentious performances, displays and campaigns by which ordinary people made collective claims on others [Tilly, 2004]. For Tilly, social movements are a major vehicle for ordinary people's participation in public politics [Tilly, 2004:3].

can mobilize. Each and every sustainable development process needs to ensure that the members feel they are worthy through their participation, attachment to the cause, involvement in the decision making process and implementation. Through providing this space and collaborating together in this journey will definitely develop unity among the members. It is equally important to have adequate representation in the local governance to ensure mobilization of resources. Therefore it is important for participation in the gram sabha and panchayat samiti. It is equally important for capable, vocal and informed decision-makers in this process who can provide critical mass towards sustainable development. All this would not be possible without the commitment to see this through to the end. Therefore it is important that we address this not only from an economic approach but from the values approach that is inclusive, participatory and transparent and accountable.

And yet through all of this, we are made aware of the power of silence as a tool for realization. When we are alone and we put aside all other forms of communication with the outside world, we are forced to communicate with ourselves and our conscience. This is a journey that few would like to undergo a painful yet re-awakening journey of self-introspection. We engage in a process of remembering, thinking and analysing our thoughts, actions and words. This is when the Greek term 'Gnothi Seauton' gains importance as this literally means 'Know thyself'. This would have to be complemented with the Latin term 'temet nosce' which means 'thine own self thou must'. These are powerful lighthouses as they have the possibility providing illumination in the parts of our lives that have been kept in the dark. In many cases we are afraid as our vulnerabilities became the weapons for those eager for our downfall. And it is at this time that we have to grapple with the contradictions, the decisions, the joys and mistakes. But in this silence lies the power to realize that potential and opportunity that we have shut out of our lives. It leads to the path of a realization of our lives in relation to those around us and also with God. Therein lies the power of silence as it quietly urges us to reach out to others only to discover ourselves. This process of awareness enables us to see ourselves through the eyes of those and pause long enough to re-position ourselves with the outside world. While we are engaging in this process of soul-searching, we are establishing a common thread that binds us through our joys, sorrows, problems and solutions with the masses. This process of silence helps us to identify the factors that include us and not alienate us.

Armchair Advocates of the Church

In my brief but varied experience, we have lost the moral right to speak for the people if we cannot be with the people. We must move from the paradigm of monuments to Christ to movements for Christ. A majority in the world of the WCC, CWM, CCA, NCCI, NGO's and theological institutions have regressed into the world of ivory tower theologians and perfectionists in the art of oration but have forgotten the essence of Christ's ministry while indulging in only their own self-preservation. The advocates of the dalits, adivasis and gender in these organizations are, in the words of another, 'controllers of ecumenism within yet another bureaucratic organization'. Sadly they are not the true representations of the people back in their own countries and have lost all contact with the communities.

Church: Challenge to Break the Silence

The silence that we have maintained, while we have watched the oppression of the poor, corruption within the church, institutions, even within our families from the sidelines continue, while we pray and wait for the Lord to act. That makes us as guilty as much as those that have oppressed or engaged in corrupt practices. During my interactions within the church circles, the now 'pre-recorded message' is that we will act tomorrow. It is another matter that tomorrow never comes for those whose just sit around waiting. It is indeed a pity that we do not transcend the boundaries of our differences and combine our forces. Why is it that we have an attack of conscience only when the deeds have long gone lost their relevance? Even the best of the best hesitate to bell the cat. I firmly believe that our Lord has called upon us to pray earnestly (not only in the confines of our homes or church and it may not always be with our eyes closed) but during our every word, thought and action. The role of the each and every person is to identify those common threads, discover their roles and join in the struggle of the oppressed. It is much easier when it is the values that bind the masses and not enter the struggle for self-interests. Our value premise lays in the fact that we have received many blessings from God that it is our moral responsibility to works towards the upliftment of those less privileged than us. The Church today is challenged to move outwards and get involved in the congregations, ward / circles, panchayats, gram sabhas. It can be something as simple as cleaning the localities, cities or joining the campaigns against the misuse of the resources in the forest areas. It could also take the form of re-inventing ourselves to become Green Church Models through our institutions, supporting the livelihoods of the adivasis and dalits in the urban/rural areas. The options are many to enter the Kingdom of God but the takers are few. Breaking the silence starts at home, in our neighbourhoods against the structural and systemic injustices that have prevailed and taken a stranglehold of our consciences.

Conclusion

I would like to conclude this with a small reference to the very beginning of a book that provides the basis of our faith, inspiration and hope, the Bible. It also includes life situations, teachings and warnings on the power of silence, development and empowerment. I would like to take us through a journey way down in history, to the beginning of time. The Book of Genesis places us at a time when the world began and it fills us with awe. Can you imagine just being given the privilege to witness the creation of the world as God went about His Creating Process with consummate ease? He created the pure air, clean water, fertile land, abundant light, innumerable species of plants and animals. Then he created humans. Ask any Sunday school child about the duration of this creation process and prompt comes the response: 6 days. What skips our attention and is of vital importance to our understanding of the power of silence in the process of creation. "God looked at everything he had made, and he was very pleased (Gen 1:31)…and he had stopped working (Gen 2:1). This is a powerful affirmation from the Creator that the creation is a self-sustaining ecosystem, beautiful and the resources within this earth are abundant. And more importantly there is a need for work to stop and silence to commence. Because in that silence lies the power to reflect, realize, align and change. We have the moral responsibility to ensure that the right to enjoy the beauty of God's creations is that of every living being. Yet the hope at the end of the road, as Christians, is that we are challenged by the work of our forefathers to carry the message of 'breaking the silence', engaging with the communities (walking, eating, sweating and sitting with them), and transforming the Silence of Oppression to the Silence emanating from Pure Joy.

Chapter - 11

'A Point of View' :
The Marginalised
of India in the 21st Century

– *Ashis Sahu*

Since economic liberalisation in the early 1990's, India has been receiving applauds on the global stage for its impressive rate of economic growth. A skilled and cost effective workforce combined with a usurping appetite for consumption from an ever increasing middle class, makes it a key business partner whether it be targeting Indian consumers and/or using India as a manufacturing or service sourcing hub. However, amidst all this economic prosperity, 75% of the population remains below the poverty line (World Bank's definition of "below the poverty line" are those unable to earn more than $365 per year). There is an urgent need to address the economic and social distress faced by those who have a voice; one that has and is crying out for help but is not being heard by most of society.

There is no doubt that by India achieving sustained economic growth, opportunities are being created for the endless graduates (and their families) that the Indian educational system churns out.

As a result, the standard of living for those who are able to secure well paying jobs has increased and due to this growth, companies are able to offer a wider range of products/services to the Indian households while at the same time the Indian Government is able to invest in building the infrastructure in India. However, one thought on the "jobs being created" is how long will graduates (a majority of them) be satisfied with taking jobs in call centres and outsourced centres. Eventually, they will want something more professionally challenging and the dynamics of how the private sector in India develops over the next 5-10 years will be interesting to observe. The bottom line is that for a significant number of the Indian population, the cycle of poverty continues to be an endless one

Varying schools of thought exist on the approach that the Indian Government needs to take in order to address the issues faced by the marginalised. Some argue that the priority should not be on economic growth but instead a conscious effort to redistribute wealth through transparent and measurable programmes that make a difference for the marginalised. Others believe that the focus should be on economic growth, as it allows increased capital to be allocated for development initiatives. Both sides have valid points. Yes, economic growth allows more capital for redistribution but getting submerged in this phenomenon of capitalism and its by-product "materialism" should be approached with a certain degree of caution.

The reasons being, the values of society change when there is an obsession around creating wealth. The sad reality is that most people don't realise the by-products of such a system, and it can be clearly seen when we look at the recent global credit crisis. The infamous banks (almost all of whom have posted record breaking profits and turned around their performance within a year) created a system whereby those who did not have good credit history could receive mortgages for houses with high interest rates. While it does not take financial expertise to realise that a product which works on such rationale is indeed risky (risk and return are directly related in the world of finance but when the risk gets transferred to unaware third parties, there is a major problem), it is the greed of the financial institutions that played a major role in the global credit crisis. Governments in Europe and America had to step in to save economies from collapsing and tax-payers money was required for the so called "bail out" packages to banks in order for them to continue to operate. For some banks it was too late while others survived and are once again, achieving record breaking profit levels.

What are the lessons to be learnt from this? One, banks need to be governed on a far better scale and national governments need to collectively to bring relevant legislation otherwise banks will merely relocate if the policies within a particular country are not favourable to them. Two, people have become so infatuated with consumerism beyond their financial means, that when businesses and financial institutions see an opportunity to exploit it, they aggressively push to connect the product/service and potential customer, regardless of the potentially damaging consequences. Unfortunately, the lessons learnt from the credit crisis have not been acted upon besides a few legislations (minimal impact in nature) on how banks will operate. In the meantime, jobs are being lost in the public and private sector, governments had to introduce cost cutting mechanisms across key sectors such as education and healthcare, small to medium businesses simply don't have the ability to meet their operational costs and are forced to shut down; a very gloomy picture indeed. I suppose the irony is that even after such a century shaking event where numerous stakeholders have been affected, it is frustrating to see the lethargic and lack-of-purpose response from governments and society as a whole to address the root cause of why this happened and to ensure that such an incident does not repeat itself.

Without digressing and coming back to the main issue on hand here, what about the plight of the poor? Poverty is prevalent across people of all faiths and regions and there is no dearth of it in India. From stepping out of a train station to visiting villages or cities, it is something that one is constantly surrounded by. A certain level of immunity is built by those who witness it, understandably so. It is not like certain parts of the world (developed nations) where if you happen to live in certain areas, only then do you witness it and nowhere near on the scale as in India. However, it is shocking to see how the rising middle class in India are fixated on owning designer clothes and imported luxury cars. It makes me wonder what must be going on in the mother's head who is begging on the side of the street in order to feed her children and for the endless hours of toil that a father puts in to feed his family with one square meal, if that. These examples may be clichéd but how much longer do the poor have to watch this endless debauchery. Losing a child because the hospitals were too far away or because treatment for basic health problems was not an option must destroy ones faith or hope in any salvation.

So, what role is society playing to help those in poverty? The common man believes it is the responsibility of the Government to drive forward initiatives to help the marginalised. Given the inherent dynamics of India, the Government has an extremely challenging task amidst numerous other challenges when trying to reduce the levels of poverty. The MNREGA (Mahatma Gandhi National Rural Employment Guarantee Scheme) is a step in the right direction which started in 2006 and seeks to provide a guaranteed 100 days of paid work to unemployed adults. A positive step indeed but how does a family manage for the remaining 265 days of the year? Irrespective of whether free education exists, a family battling for survival will look at how to maximise their earning capacity in the short term and this means making their children work and in turn sacrificing education. This is the harsh dilemma that many are faced with and one that results in the likelihood of the next generation being held captive at the bottom of society.   The Government might want to explore how we can create a welfare system. Successful models of welfare systems can be found in the West and understanding these and customising it to the Indian system would be extremely beneficial for the nation's future. It is by no means an easy task but there are think tanks, academics, non-for profit organisations that have explored and advocate such a concept in India but practical implementation can be a tiresome task when working through the endless levels of bureaucracy and infinite third parties working solely on self-interest.

If one has not seen the plight of the poor, then it can't necessarily be expected for them to act but if one has seen and not acted, that is definitely questionable on a moral front. The struggles of the poor in India are prevalent in all aspects of daily life. Society needs to build a moral conscience and play a more direct role in trying to making a difference for the poor. Simply donating money to charities and volunteering time amidst our hectic schedules is not enough. The parameters of how most define success in the 21st century seem to be very empty in meaning. Does a trader in an investment bank who makes bets that a company's share price will go up or down and in turn picks up six figure bonuses play a more important role in society than the social worker in a village working with the marginalised amidst testing circumstances? The answer is relatively straightforward and while I don't expect social workers to be paid on par with bankers, the difference in pay raises numerous questions. We as a society need to change this mentality whereby those trying to make a difference for the marginalised should be compensated fairly in order to bring the right talent for without the right leadership and constituents within the team, development efforts on this front can stagnate and become a painful process to watch.

Leadership is a vital component in determining whether efforts and initiatives to reduce inequalities is a successful one or not. So, what can the Church in India do on this front? First step is to actually have people with leadership abilities and potential in the right positions. Those who have vision, sound principles, are able to lead teams towards a common goal and are driven by the desire to make a positive difference need to be the future Church leaders in whatever capacity. Unfortunately, what one finds is a lack of the above characteristics and as this is the case, how will organisations and the Church move forward. It is very disheartening to see inarticulate leaders who are more concerned about making their commissions through various entrepreneurial ventures (in the loosest sense of the word) and act with total disregard of why they joined the "ministry" in the first place. The mere hypocrisy of having to listen to a sermon from a person who practices the opposite of what he preaches does not bode well for building honesty and a sense of community within the Church.

Likewise, those leading non-for profits need to take into account their team members needs instead of living a private sector lifestyle of a Chief Executive (the only difference being there is less emphasis on accountability) and be conscious of the sacrifices their employees make. If one does not create and foster a strong bond within a team, achieving goals can become an arduous task. The lack of effective leadership results in compromising the quality and extent of delivering successful initiatives to the poor. There are numerous people in Churches, academic institutions, non-for-profits that work with unquestionable commitment amidst trying circumstances, a lot of times not only for themselves but for their families as well. It is heartening to see such a selfless way of working and living for others while making numerous sacrifices along the way.

The time has come whereby there is a need for a collective approach that needs to be taken by those who want to make a difference for the marginalised. Society needs to understand its duty and responsibilities to making a difference for the marginalised. Like minded individuals that want to bring and see change, who are selfless in their approach and demonstrate ethically and morally sound principles need to be identified and supported so that they can lead organisations and address the needs of the marginalised. In the worlds pursuit of embracing technology and securing a better lifestyle (whatever that means), one needs to spare a thought and act for those that are being left behind in this cattle race. It has never been and will not be an easy path to walk. Amidst all the barriers that one encounters from a society that barely has a social conscience to supposed leaders both in the Church and development field that have an agenda based on mere self interest, there is still hope for each person that believes and acts to make a difference for impoverished, a small and stronger step is being taken in the right direction. Transformations do not take place overnight especially when trying to change people's perception and views on issues but creating a community of individuals who believe in improving the lives of those in poverty provides a platform for solidarity and support as we embark on a difficult journey knowing that gradually, change can be brought about. The sound of silence allows for introspection and can be the ignition required to make an effort to bring about change. My sincere prayer is that change can and will be brought so that the cries of the marginalised will be heard and acted upon.

Chapter - 12

Issues of Stewardship in the 'Church Today' : A Call to Responsible Governance

Sanjay Patra

Church as a body of Christ is Committed to effective management of resources. In both Mathew chapter 14 about feeding of 5000 and chapter 15 of feeding the 4000, Lord Jesus Christ himself demonstrated the value of good stewardship by asking his disciples to collect the leftovers in large baskets. A point of reference can be the Church of North India Constitution section-II, part-II which speaks about the objects and purposes.

*"The Objects and Purposes of the Church of North India, operating through its Synod, Dioceses and Pastorates, shall be to proclaim by word and deed the gospel of Jesus Christ, who is the lord and the Master of the Church, for the salvation and good of all humankind through unity witness and service which may include educational, medical , social, agricultural and other services and also through worship and other activities of the Church which promote spiritual growth, **self reliance**, social justice and moral regeneration, irrespective of caste , creed or color." (Page 40)*

It can be seen above that self reliance is a major ingredient in the objects and purpose of CNI. Likewise many main line churches as well as other smaller groups aspire to become self reliant. One cannot be fully self reliant so long as the financial self reliance is not ensured.

Through this paper, we will be looking at the finance management and stewardship from the following perspectives:

- Financial Accountability and Integrity
- Stewardship
- Self Reliance
- Property Issues
- Governance

1.1. Financial Accountability and Integrity

In 2-Corinthians 8, Paul advises the Church at Corinth for the proper handling and distribution of Church funds- and the need to do so in honest and accountable way. The members of the Corinth community were collecting a substantial offering to be distributed to the poor in distant Jerusalem. Paul assures them that Titus, whom they knew to be a man of integrity, and another highly regarded man (unnamed in the text) had been "chosen by the Churches to accompany us as we carry the offering" (2 Corinthians 8:19).

Paul also mentions a third Christian Brother, a man with equally impeccable credentials, who would watch over the carrying of the funds. Titus and these two men, who were to join Paul and his group, formed a company to be trusted in handling and distributing the offerings (2 Corinthians 8:22-23).

Paul assures the Corinthians that his group would administer the funds: in order to honour the Lord and to show their eagerness to help (2 Corinthians 8:19). Paul welcomed the direct participation of the other two trusted men of sound character overseeing the funds. In fact, it is likely he initiated their involvement.

Any Church that resists financial accountability creates suspicion. Paul says, "We want to avoid any criticism of the way we administer this liberal gift" (2 Corinthians 8:20). He went out of his way to include other trusted men of integrity -both from inside and outside his group.

Paul also says, "We are taking pains to do what is right, not only in the eyes of the Lord but also in the eyes of people" (2 Corinthians 8:21). Here two important safeguards for preserving financial integrity and accountability are implied:

First we need to take pains to do what is right. A system of financial accountability may seem awkward, time-consuming, or a nuisance. At times it may seem unnecessary. But, it is right, and therefore we must take pains to establish proper checks and balances.

Second, it's not enough to say, "Our conscience is clear before the Lord." Our actions must be above reproach, " not only in the eyes of the Lord but also in the eyes of people.." whatever system of collecting and distributing funds we choose, it must involve transparency and accountability, with a plurality of men or women approved of integrity and character (preferably not chosen by each other but by a Church or constituency). Although two most qualified family members might appropriately sit together on the board, there's no place for the sort of nepotism that makes some Churches top-heavy with under-qualified relatives and childhood friends who look the other way instead of fostering accountability.

A telling questions to ask in any Church or ministry is this: Who has the courage and authority to tell the decision makers that what they are doing is right or wrong?

Therefore the following key ingredients for good financial management and stewardship are:

- To ensure transparency by involving more people

- By allowing more questioning
- Be open by setting up system and processes for clear decision making
- Avoiding conflict of interest by setting up policies

We need to follow all of these so that we not only are accountable but we also appear accountable.

1.2. Stewardship

Good stewardship means to be faithful in giving what rightfully belongs to the Lord and at the same time administering it in an accountable manner. As a community of God's people, the blessing of giving for His Church is of very high importance. Someone said "Giving is not giving until it hurts". At the same time the value of using the collected funds for the right purpose need to be emphasized. We need to understand that people (be it individual or groups or institutions both within the country and abroad) give sacrificially for the Kingdom of God. That puts a lot of responsibility on the Church that administers this gift.

Another important area that we need to keep in perspective is that the giving or stewardship cannot be looked at in isolation. It has a deep connection with the spiritual life of the Church. In fact our giving reflects the spiritual condition.

Bible says:

"Will a man rob God? Yet you have robbed me! But you say, "In what way have we robbed you?" In tithes and offerings ....Bring all the tithes into the store house, that there may be food in my house. And try me now in this. Says the Lord of hosts. "If I will not open for you the windows of heaven and pour out for you such blessing that there will not be room enough to receive it" Malachi 3:8, 10

That is a great trial of affliction the abundance of their joy and their deep poverty abounded in the riches of their liberality. For I bear witness that according t their ability. Yes and beyond their ability they were freely willing, imploring us with much urgency that we would receive the gift and the fellowship of the ministering to the saints. (2 Corinthians 8:2)

Further an important issue to be kept in mind about stewardship is that a Church exists for others and not for herself. We need to introspect and ask the question "What and for whom do we exist?" That should be reflected in our budget. We need to examine our budget to see if our mission program is dominant in the funds outlay? Or are we in the maintenance mode by only meeting the cost of our existence?

As a Church, it is important to emphasize very much on the stewardship aspects so that we can be a sharing community willing to live out the good news. One of the areas to be critically looked at would be the focus on stewardship in our Churches, and other institutions who exist and uphold the name of Jesus Christ.

1.3. Self Reliance

As stated above, the object and purposes of "self reliance" is a means to proclaim by word and deed the gospel of Jesus Christ. Therefore the issue of "self reliance" is at the core of the ministry of church.

Mahatma Gandhi once said that the key to self reliant India lies in self reliant villages. A parallel can be drawn in Church Management and can be said that self reliant local churches would contribute to a self reliant national church.

The issue of foreign funds vis-à-vis Indian fund raising has been a major issue for a long time in our churches. For a long time, the issue of getting financially self-reliant is being strongly raised and discussed at various forums of the churches. The issue of self reliance needs to be addressed at three levels viz:

a.　Congregation/Pastorate Level
b.　Diocesan Level
c.　Synod Level

1.3.1. Congregation/Pastorate Level

At this level, the basic source of revenue is through giving of people. Apart from that, there are some other income in form of sale of souvenirs, special events etc. The nature of expenses can be both administrative as well as programmatic. In fact the staff salaries must also be built into the budget. Our dream would be to see all the pastorates self-reliant.

1.3.2. Diocesan Level

At this level the main source of revenue (should be) is assessment from pastorates. However, it has been seen that in most of the Dioceses, the source of revenue has been from institutions, rent, lease etc. Very little income has been generated through assessments. The main area of expenditure has been for administration, salaries and other program expenses. The challenge is to move our diocesan reliance from institutions/ other funding to funding through assessments.

1.3.3. Synod Level

At Synod level the main income source is interest from endowments. The assessment from Dioceses which should form a major part of Synod funds is unfortunately not there and so the Synod has to depend on the external grants and endowments. On one hand the grants are reducing as global economy is changing, rupee getting stronger etc. and on the other the interest rates are falling thereby making the endowment income less. Further, the costs are increasing in terms of salaries and others.

The above scenario poses the question to us, "Are we / will we be financially viable as a Church?" what concrete steps we need to take to make it a financially viable Church? What about the financially weaker and relatively stronger Dioceses? How are the common resources shared?

1.4. Property Issues

Our churches have been blessed with a lot of properties many of which were inherited from former denominations, mission boards etc.

The whole area of property development, alienation and addition also needs to be streamlined. There is a need to have an absolute transparent process in public for any property to be sold. Right now, in most case, the property dealings within churches alienates the local people. Care needs to be taken to make the property dealing transparent at the local level also.

Churches have to emerge with a clear plan as to development of their properties. Like in the parable of talents, we need to put it to the best use for the glory of God. Churches need to first prepare an overall inventory of all the properties, their status and further development plan. This plan should be an inclusive plan (with local people). It also needs to be ensured that the sale proceeds of the properties which are capital receipts should be utilized for capital expenditures and not for revenue expenditure.

1.5. Governance

The Jethro principle as given in Exodus 18:21 says, "But select capable men from all the people-men who fear God, trustworthy men who hate dishonest gain- and appoint them as officials over thousands, hundreds, fifties and tens"

It describes the characteristics required for people who would govern. They are to:

- **Be capable** – We need people with professional competence

- **Be from all people** – We need good representation i.e men, women, different language groups, ethnicity etc.

- **Fear God** – People who put God first in their life

- **Be trustworthy** – A very important trait is to have high integrity

- **Hate dishonest gain** – Financial/material honesty

A tall order indeed. How many of our church leaders would match up to these qualities to-day? There is a need for introspection of the present day church leaders to-day in the light of above principle.

In the New Testament, Jesus gave a new paradigm to leadership and governance by "Servant Leadership".

"Those who are supposed to rule over the Gentiles lord it over them, and their great men exercise authority over them," Jesus said to his disciples, "but it shall not be so among you!" Rather than being lords, he went on to say, disciples are to be servants of one another and the greatest is the one who is servant of all (Mark 10:42-43).

By these words Jesus indicates that an entirely different system of governance than that employed by the world should prevail among Christians. Authority among Christians is not derived from the same source as worldly authority, nor is it to be exercised in the same manner. The world's view of authority places people over one another, as in a military command structure, a business executive hierarchy, or a governmental system. This is as it should be. Urged by the competitiveness created by the Fall, and faced with the rebelliousness and ruthlessness of sinful human nature, the world could not function without the use of command structures and executive decision.

But as Jesus carefully stated, "...it shall not be so among you." Disciples are always in a different relationship to one another than that of the world. Christians are brothers and sisters, children of one Father, and members of one family. Jesus put it clearly in Matthew 23:8, "One is your Master, and all you are brethren."

Throughout twenty centuries the church has virtually ignored these words. Probably with the best of intentions, it has nevertheless repeatedly borrowed in totality the authority structures of the world, lording it over the brethren and thus destroying the model of servanthood which our Lord intended. Christians have so totally forgotten Jesus' words that they frequently have set up the world's pattern of governance without bothering to change the names, and have operated churches, mission organizations, youth organizations, schools, colleges, and seminaries, all in the name of Jesus Christ, but with presidents, directors, managers, heads and chiefs in no way different from corresponding secular structures.

It is probably too late to do much about altering the many structures , but certainly Jesus' words must not be ignored in the worship and training functions of the church itself. Somewhere, surely, the words of Jesus, "...it shall not be so among you," must find some effect. Yet in most churches today an unthinking acceptance has been given to the idea that the ordained minister is the final voice of authority in both doctrine and practice, and that he is the executive officer of the church with respect to administration.

It is clear from the scriptures that the apostles were concerned about the danger of developing ecclesiastical bosses. In 2 Corinthians 1:24 Paul reminds the Corinthians concerning his own apostolic authority, "...not that we lord it over your faith; we work with you for your joy..." In the same letter he describes, with apparent disapproval, how the Corinthians reacted to certain leaders among themselves: "For you bear it if a man makes slaves of you, or preys upon you, or takes advantage of you, or puts on airs, or strikes you in the face" (2 Corinthians 11:20). Peter, too, is careful to warn the elders (and he includes himself among them) not to govern by being "...domineering over those in your charge, but being examples to the flock." And John speaks strongly against Diotrephes "who likes to put himself first, and takes it on himself to put some out of the church." These first-century examples of church bosses indicate how easily churches then (as in the 20th century) ignored the words of Jesus, "it shall not be so among you."

But if the church is not to imitate the world in this matter, what is it to do? Leadership must certainly be exercised within the church and there must be some form of authority. What is it to be? The question is answered in Jesus' words: "One is your Master." All too long churches have behaved as if Jesus were far away in heaven and he has left it up to church leaders to make their own decisions and run their own affairs. But Jesus himself had assured them in giving the Great Commission, "Lo, I am with you always, even unto the end of the age." And in Matthew 18:20 he reiterated, "Where two or three are gathered together in my name, there am I in the midst of them." Clearly this indicates that he is present not only in the church as a whole but in every local church as well. It is Jesus himself, therefore, who is the ultimate authority within every body of Christians, and he is quite prepared to exercise his authority through the instrument he himself has ordained—the eldership.

Christ gives example after example through His Life and Words about the church governance that He desires for the body of His elect! First in Mat. 20: 25-26, Christ commands and teaches His disciples by giving them a lesson in church governance, that is to be exercised through **service and humility.** Christ says, *"You know that the princes (leaders) of the Gentiles (unbelievers) exercise dominion over them, and they that are great exercise authority upon them."* Christ tells His disciples that this is the way the leadership of the world govern their people, that they lord it over their people, by exercising a top down chain of authority over them, as a hierarchy, or an oligarchy.

This is the way all of the world leaders govern their people. Christ in verse 26 says, ...*"But it shall not be so among you (the church); but whosoever will be great among you* (who desires to be great by being over others in the church), *let him be your minister (servant)." Verse 27, "and whosoever will be chief among you, let him be your servant."* In verse 27, Christ then gave His own example as an example for leaders to follow when He said, " He came not to be ministered unto, but to minister—serve by example, and to give His life a ransom for many."

Christ gave another governance example when He said the Kingdom of God, and entrance into His Kingdom is through having the heart of a little child, Mat. 19: 14, and Mat. 18: 3-4. Are these verses just for the "lowly" brethren, or is this teaching for all, including the "exalted" ministers? Children don't have a heart and mind of being a dictator over one another, but are humble and meek. Christ said this humble heart and mind is required to enter the Kingdom of God. Many of the ministers of the Churches of God must believe that they can enter God's Kingdom not having the heart of a little child as Christ taught, but having their "exalted" positions of authority, as hierarchists, by exalting themselves over the "lowly" brethren. They don't serve the brethren from positions of abasing themselves in order to serve the brethren, as humble examples of a servant. Another example of Christ, that He set before the church was that of washing the disciples' feet, John 13. Even though our spiritual leaders keep the symbolic feet washing service every year, do they exercise this service in their relationship with each other the rest of the year?

The apostle Paul and others set the example of humility, service and working for their own needs in the New Testament church. Paul served the church and did not set himself up to be served. Where is this awesome example being exercised by ministers today? Peter exhorts the elders to serve as overseers, watching over the members' spiritual growth and safety, pointing out false ministers, and not to serve as hirelings, working for and worshipping money, but willing and ready, and not serving as lords (hierarchists) over the church, but being examples to the flock, I

Peter 5: 1-3. The teaching that says "God resists the proud and gives grace to the humble," falls on deaf ears in the ministry of the churches.

Why do the hierarchists of the Churches behave as they do? It is because they believe that God's Word in Hebrews 13 gives them Scripture for their top-down ruler ship of authority in the church, where it says, "having the rule over you" means to them a hierarchical rule, Heb. 13: 7, Heb. 13: 17, and Heb. 13: 24. The word rule in these verses means, as an overseer, and Peter gives this as the meaning and understanding to the elders, I Peter 5: 1-3, not as being lords (elders of exalted rank and authority), but living examples of God's way of love and service to the flock.

How does God desire to govern His church ? God desires to govern His saints through the power of His Holy Spirit. Study I John 2: 26-27. John was an excellent example of being an overseer of the flock, and not exalting himself as a hierarchist, and not even mentioning and exalting his own name in his writings. Today ministers not only exalt their names, but their families and everything about them. In these verses John, as an overseer in verse 26, is warning the members about those who are deceiving church ministers and teachers that will seduce the saints into believing certain teachings that are not in the Scriptures, and in verse 27, he says, ***"But the anointing (God's Spirit) which you have received of Him abides in you, and you need not that any man teach you: but as the same anointing teaches you of all things, and is truth, and is no lie, and even as it has taught you, you shall abide in him."*** Christ said, *"His Words are spirit, and they are life,"* John 6:63. Some of today's ministers believe that their words are spirit and life and if you don't follow them and their organization, you will fail and lose out in salvation.

1.6. Conclusion

Christianity started out in Palestine as a relationship; it moved to Greece and became a philosophy; it moved to Italy and became an institution; it moved to Europe and became a culture; it came to America and became an enterprise and in India it became projects and programmes. It is important to come back to the basic issue – relationship with Christ.

Christ desires to lead, govern, and rule every saint through the power of His Holy Spirit. God's Holy Spirit is the helper, sent from God to help His people, John 14:16. A minister, as a servant of God, and if God's Spirit really dwells in and leading him, can also be a helper to the saints in their rule over members, meaning to supervise them as an overseer, and not as an overlord. The "man ordained" ministers of today are led by the flesh, and not by God's Spirit. They then create a power structure in the church, that they call a church hierarchy, where they try to rule over God's sheep by the ways of flesh, which is with cruelty and rigor, through their policies and laws of the flesh, instead of directing the brethren to Christ and His Spirit. This results in dishonesty, nepotism and corruption. May the church of God and its leaders wake up to this call.

Chapter - 13

A Walk to Remember

Surendra Sahu

It is my privilege and honour to write a personal memoir on the occasion of the sixtieth birthday of Bishop Dhirendra Kumar Sahu. He tried his best to be a faithful servant of his Master Lord and Saviour Jesus Christ and tried to follow the examples set by our father, the Late Rev Birendra Kumar Sahu. The beginning was very humble and non-descript. Birendra Kumar Sahu was born in a remote village of Bhusandpur in Orissa and grew up in Khurda town of Orissa state under the care of his widowed mother Netramani Sahu. His mother was a Hindu by religion but had to leave the village after being tortured by her family members. She came out from the village with her son and stayed in 'Christian Sahi' in Khurda town and served a few families as a house-helper. Thereafter she became the saxton of Khurda Baptist Church. Birendra Sahu managed an education only up to middle school and thereafter chose to be a tailor as this would provide a source of income for his family. He took over the responsibility of saxton from his mother and served the Church as his mother grew old. His mother accepted Jesus Christ as her personal Saviour and was baptized in the same church. She was soon to be followed by her son. While serving the house of the Lord, he was moved by a call to ministry and did a short course in theological training and became the Honorary Pastor of Khurda Baptist Church. He served the church as honorary pastor for thirty three years with the tailoring profession as the source of income for his family. He set an example of tent making ministry (serving the Lord while earning an income from another profession) in the 1950's in a state having 2% of Christian population. He was married to Pramodini Sahu and was blessed with five sons Dhirendra, Surendra, Prasant, Dilip and Pradeep. The credit for making a home and making guests feel at home would rest solely on her shoulders. The fruits of his labour led to the distinction of being known in Orissa as the 'Barefoot Pastor'. Simplicity, Commitment, firm faith in God and most importantly prayerful life was an integral part of his life and ministry.

Through his hard labour five churches were planted in Nayagarh district of Orissa. His vision was to preach the gospel and passion for pastoral care of the marginalized in any place at any time and in any circumstances was commendable. He reached out to people of other faiths in nearby villages and towns with the gospel through his leadership and efforts. The pastoral ministry of fulfilling the needs of the people who were deprived of such care was not only regular but also an integral part of his calling. He walked several miles to reach those families and visited the rural congregations to serve the Lord and the society. The barefoot pastor pressed on toward the goal for the prize of the heavenly call of God in Christ Jesus and went to be with his Master on 3rd January 1998. His lifetime companion was to join him 7 years later on 9th June 2005.

The Barefoot Pastor had dedicated his first child from his wife's womb to serve the Lord. He is none other than Bishop Dhirendra Kumar Sahu who followed the footsteps of his father and walked in difficult paths to serve God's purpose in his generation. Looking back on the paths that he has followed, one can only be grateful to

God for His protection and blessings. He has always admitted that it is only the grace of God that has enabled him to be a witness in a wider circle but never forgetting his roots. The burden for rural ministry remains in his heart as a challenge and an opportunity. The profile of the same person in this volume speaks the multifaceted character of a servant of God and the significant contribution to the life of the universal church. The pastoral ministry in Kondhmal district of Orissa within the then Diocese of Cuttack in the Church of North India, along with eighteen years of teaching and administration in Serampore College, his Episcopal ministry in the Diocese of Eastern Himalaya, the General Secretary of the National Council of Churches in India reflects his ecumenical spirit.

The blessing of having eldest son Bibhudutta, daughter-in-law Natashia, grand-daughters Aavisha and Davinia and the youngest son Ashis is a life of contentment that can only be grateful to God. He has remained as one whose horizons have always rooted in Christ and who continues to walk humbly with God ....

He is like a father-figure to all of me, having helped me to acquire a good education and sound advice on developing my career. He was an advisor who nurtured me through the theological studies. I remember the days during 1965-67 when he used to earn money through tuitions in order to support my studies alongside his ongoing studies. His footsteps remain an inspiration for the next generation in our family as he walked with total faith in God. In the years 1971-72 he was called to Rourkela to preach the word of God along with his father. It was the first time that I got an opportunity to accompany him. It was during this visit that I began to understand evangelism and ministry. He used to walk for miles and visit all the melas and went about distributing tracks without any complaint. He was the inspiration behind my decision to join the ministry.

– Surendra Kumar Sahu (brother)

After the demise of our father, Bhai took on the role as the head of the family. It was not a sudden shift but one that began during his early days when we were still students. We recognize his decisions as he was always thinking about us and our children. His simplicity was his outstanding feature in spite of his academic credentials. During the time of his exams, his college had a reputation for its students engaging in unfair practices. It was widely known that no one in the college would pass with flying colors without copying. The principal and staff were confounded as bhai did not engage in any unfair means during the exams. He was a witness to his faith and belief and confounded them further by acquiring a 1st class in the exams. He had a queue of institutions requesting him to join them but he was determined to follow in his father's footsteps and continue in the ministry. He stayed true to his father's wish that his eldest son would join the ministry. Even today, the professors speak highly of him due to his principles and practices.

– Prasant Kumar Sahu (Brother)

He was very honest, sincere and fully prepared towards his responsibilities as a theology teacher. His discipline and ability to relate to the students was noteworthy. From 1983-86, he was my theology teacher and then my guide for my thesis studies. I have learned a lot about human values and his work ethic. He has an ocean of knowledge in his respective field that very few could match up to. During my time as a student he was my advisor and guided me in the right spirit.

– Rt. Rev. Samson Das (Diocese of Cuttack, C.N.I)

He is man to look up to because during the time that our fathers grew up, he was the first to take the steps to shoulder the responsibilities of the family both financially and physically. He made the family proud by being one the few to study Theology at Oxford University. There are two outstanding qualities: he has maintained his simplicity even as he was seated in the highest places and does not forget the people around him. He fought all his battles in his life not with anger but with belief and composure. Even during the tough and trying times at NCCI, there were people who supported him due to his simplicity and his methodology of work. I am proud to be known as the nephew of Bishop Sahu within the church circles. He always keeps in mind the basic principles of Christianity and service to God.

– Sourav Sahu (Nephew)

He is cool because we can talk about current issues, debates on TV or maybe an article in the newspaper. He is easy going and can relate to any age group. Sometimes he gives me advice and shows genuine interest in my career and life choices. He loves to have coffee in the cafe's as well as read books. During all his visits to Bangalore, there has always been someone who would stop to chat with him during his walks on M. G. Road in Bangalore. He seems to know more people than us even though he is not a resident of Bangalore. I was touched by his sermons that emphasized that you need not be rich or an intellectual to do good for others. Just be yourself, reach out and touch people's lives.

– Namrata Sahu (Niece)

After the demise of our father, he is doing the job like a father figure by caring for all of his siblings and their families. He is a good Samaritan of the modern age.

– Dilip Kumar Sahu (Brother)

He was my tutor and still behaves as though he is my tutor. His simplicity and polite nature were the qualities that attracted me to him. He is a very strong and determined person and he cannot compromise on the principles that he has set for himself. He is also like any other human who needs care, attention and support.

– Manjusree Sahu (Wife)

He is known for his Simplicity, soft-spoken nature and was more of a fatherly figure. He remains a cordial person who allows one the freedom to work and suggest positive ways of re-working the papers, programs etc. He would always engage in moulding me into a thinker. The relationship was developed on the understanding of reciprocity. We were able to share our views. He is very committed to the cause that he takes up. He is an achiever as he is drawn to the goal, task and cause.

There was an occasion during the preparations for the Human Sexuality program that I was threatened and pressure was building on him to remove me. He made me to think about the program through the eyes of the church, its ethos and theology and not that of an NGO. If there was anybody else, I would have been made to tender an apology but he assisted me so as to write differently so that the program got a positive reaction.

– Christopher Rajkumar (NCCI)

He is a good and helpful person who is sensitive to the needs of each and every member of the family. He goes out of his way to make each person feel comfortable when he is around.

– Natashia Kharkongor (daughter-in-law)

He is my grandfather. When he talks I feel nice, he gives me things that I like and buys many gifts for me. He loves me a lot and he says a lot of nice things about God. I love him because he is good to me.

– Aavisha Kharkongor (Grand-daughter)

He is a highly educated and intellectual person with a proven ability in administration. He is a teacher and a preacher with a strong pastoral approach. His sermons are well appreciated as they portray the contextual problems. He is by nature a very simple man who takes people along with him during the process of problem solving. He is a strong believer in dialogue.

– Rt. Rev. P. Dupare (Diocese of Nagpur, C.N.I)

He is a theologian and till the time that i worked with him I was enjoying my work. His understanding and relating with the reality of the community was very strong as he had internalized the problems of his people. In Eastern Himalaya Diocese, even the best administrator would have a tough time to handle the situation, but he managed to do a set a lot of things right. He is very approachable and never exuded any airs of hierarchy. I could confide in him with my official and personal problems and seek his advice. His commitment and urge to do something for the diocese inspired me to do the same for the DBSS and my people.

– Sudeep Tigga (Coordinator- Program
Facilitation Team, CNI-SBSS)

I see him as a theologian par excellence. When he became the Bishop of Eastern Himalaya Diocese, it was privilege to know him better. He used to pour himself into guiding the C.N.I and was not partial to certain people but looked at the overall growth of the C.N.I. that was why he was chosen for the post of General Secretary, N.C.C.I. he helped me immensely when I was the Moderator of the C.N.I especially during the 11th Synod in St. Stephen's College when he helped to interpret the C.N.I understanding of consecration and ordination in the right manner. I owe him a lot as he has saved my face on more than one occasion. When everybody was pressuring me to remove the then General Secretary and Treasurer of CNI, he helped me find the old minutes and prevent the removal of the persons based on sound principles and existing facts. I hold him in high regard and have continued my friendship with him.

– Rt. Rev. J. Terom (Former Moderator of C.N.I)

When I first heard him, I found him to be a good preacher and Bible study leader. If fact I would take the credit for introducing him to the C.N.I in the various workshops, Bible studies. As an individual he is friendly, accessible, close and intimate. He never maintained a distance even after becoming a Bishop. I have pleasant memories of our travels to Andaman & Nicobar Islands as we had spent close to 2 weeks there. I would say that our friendship increased after he became the General Secretary of the NCCI.

– Rev. Dr. E. D. Pradhan (General Secretary, C.N.I)

As a human being, I always felt that he is an honest, dedicated and sincere person. When I was reluctant to gain an admission as an engineering student in 1979, my brother played a pivotal role of advisor and forced me to continue with my studies. My concerns were largely borne out of the fact that our father could not support my studies and my interests were leaning towards the science stream. But my bhai assured me that he would send Rs 200/- pm (it was a lot at that time) till I complete my studies. I remain indebted to him for forcing me to continue with my studies as an engineer.

– Pradip Kumar Sahu (Brother)

Epilogue
Dhirendra Kumar Sahu

Reminiscences

One of the easiest ways to see God's will for our lives is to look at retrospectively, as though through a rear view mirror. It is much easier to see his movements in our lives when we reflect on the journey behind us rather than try to predict what he plans for the future. Looking back, we often see clearly how something that did not make any sense at all at that time has proven to be indispensable. Looking at life personally in retrospect seems to be a dream come true. Recalling those moments not only makes me humble but also ever grateful to God. The dream of my parents as well as mine were to fulfil the call to be a fulltime minister of God when completing even the undergraduate studies in economics appeared to be unrealistic. It was a sense of achievement in 1975 when my ordination as a Presbyter of the Church of North India in the Diocese of Cuttack as well as beginning a journey with my life partner to walk together was not just coincident but providential. There has not been a moment of regret in following Jesus of Nazareth as Lord and Saviour.

The exposure to rural ministry in the Kondhmal district of Orissa was a milestone in setting the values and sharpening the perspectives of theology learnt in the confines of the classroom.

Initially it was exigent but to express solidarity with the people at that level was a learning process of theologizing. It was also an identity crisis in the sociological scenario of the context because the unanswered question is: why do our former social identities play a pivotal role in power struggle that we are supposed to have overcome after being united with Christ?

It is possible to become reclusive when betrayed but it is amazing to learn in those moments how wonderful it is to feel the sustaining power of God that overwhelms you. Stabbed behind and betrayed by the ones trusted most has been the painful experience in the last two years of journey with the National Council of Churches in India. But the amazing part is the discovery of the warmth of love, friendship and winning the respect of the people. The love and affection of the people in the pews is quite amazing. It is not possible to get rid of the ecumenical jokers and brokers as they are not a true representation of the church in the image of God. The days of armchair ecumenism are numbered and the rainfall of statements by the professional paid ecumenists is obsolete. The continuing living witness to Christ by the faithful through worship and service in the midst of adverse situations is the ecumenism where relationship with God and neighbour plays a pivotal role.

Friendship and hospitality has been the most rewarding experience during the journey which is priceless. The warmth of love of the family both nucleus and extended, the friends, the students and members of the congregations have been a constant source of encouragement and strength. The loving memories of those people who walked a second mile that enabled me along with my family to go to Oxford twice for studies. They have done it without blowing the trumpet. It has been a blessing to have a caring home where everybody is given a space to grow but basic Christian values are nurtured.

Listening to God and Listening to each other requires patience. It is becoming extremely difficult in an age of higher technology.

Speed is becoming the answer to our lives. But subordinating to the will of God requires a committed and disciplined life. It is worth reminding a saying that 'defeat is the distance between a bedtime story and a wake-up call. The former starts with once upon a time and lulls you to sleep. The second is an energizer that addresses a fresh dawn. Let me conclude with the prayer of George Matheson "I have thanked you a thousand times for my roses, but not once for my thorns. I have been looking forward to a world where I shall get compensation for my cross: but never thought of my cross as itself a present glory"

With thanks for the Prayers of the many silent ones

A Commemoration Service Address

Telling the Truth and Living the Truth

> Enlarge the place of your tent, and let the curtains of your habitations be stretched out; hold not back, lengthen your cords and strengthen your stakes. (Isaiah 54:2)

Dear sisters & brothers in Christ Jesus

We are gathered here today to commit to memory the story of Serampore trio: William Carey, Joshua Marshman and William Ward in order to 'indwell the story' which means not only inhabiting it but enacting it in our ministerial formation. We are grateful to God to be together at Tamilnadu Theological Seminary, one of the premier institutions of our family, focusing on a perspective as a cutting-edge for 'thinking and doing'. My sincere thanks to the Master of the Council, President, Registrar & members of the Senate, Principal of Serampore College, Secretary & Members of the Board for kind invitation to address this august body. I cherish the memories of eighteen years of association excluding the student period with the Theology Department of Serampore College, being privileged to live in Carey House and a space in story of Serampore (2006) but wish that the editor could have been little more generous than just one short sentence. Association with the Senate of Serampore continues for the last twenty five years and I deem it a privilege and honor to give the address. It is rightly said 'better late than never'!

Story Telling

A story is told about Menno Simons, one of the founders of Mennonite tradition. He was often pursued by the authorities who wanted to try him for heresy and burn him. Once he was travelling by coach-on the roof because all the seats inside had already been taken. It was halted by armed men on horseback. 'Is Menno Simons in there?', they shouted. Menno looked inside and asked, 'Is Menno Simons in there?' The passengers said no. So he turned to the armed men and said, 'They say he is not in there'. The armed men rode off and Menno Simons survived. The Mennonite Confession of faith today reads that 'We commit ourselves to tell the truth, to give a simple yes or no'.

Telling the truth and living the truth today is not easy in a time of deception: 'cover-up' 'fraud', 'scam'. In many professions deceptions is taken for granted and justification is given in terms of greater good. Often talked about is the politics of our time. Vinay Lal comments that the top-notch Indian politicians are essentially geriatric because of two reasons: Politics is largely based on patronage networks and takes a long time to become familiar and, is something like an afterthought, something you do after exhausting other possibilities (Indian, 22nd Dec,08). But to me politics is a reflection of the morals of our constituencies. The issue is complex and an oversimplification would be to ask a counter question under what circumstances we are allowed to tell lie? We ought to be 'truthful persons- living the truth' so that we may be capable of telling truth. In other words truth-telling should be a way of life.

Story is an essential part of our self-identity. We live in a world of stories that we are how we came to be here and of ourselves. It is a treasure house of memory that transcends the boundary of time and still speaks. The educational role of story is to challenge our presuppositions and upset our complacencies and illuminate our imaginations with new truth. Linking with the experience of the past is liberative. The people in difficult situations have found comfort by the song of the ancient Hebrew exiles 'By the waters of Babylon there we sat down, yea we wept when we remembered Zion….' (Psalm137). The dream of slaves for freedom was encapsulated and had a powerful liberative force through the story of crossing of Red Sea by the Israelites despite the disputed theories of crossing of Red Sea.

The story of God's engagements is recorded in the Old Testament. Abraham has become the archetype of all who accept the call to go out into the unknown. How we can understand and comprehend when a cobbler called William Carey said to have heard a call to come to India to preach the gospel to the heathens. But the same can not be equated with a modern day tribe of Non-Resident Indian Pastors/Theologians/ Ecumenists who also claim to have a call to make every effort to migrate from India to the comfort zones of our world. The call to serve in India has a tale. Timothy Gorringe, a former lecturer in theology at Tamil Nadu Theological Seminary, in his book 'Redeeming Time" tells, "To do theology in India is not to do theology at 120 F', as it has been romantically described, but to take part in a struggle between death and life". (Deut.30:19)

The story of all our stories finds culmination and significance in the story of the Jesus of Nazareth. His obedience to the Father and his son ship was indeed unique. The story of the passion manifests the very God in all mystery of divine love. We have a story to tell to the nations that abiding truth is mediated through the story of birth, death and resurrection of Jesus of Nazareth. The analytical skills of critical scholarship that one goes through in a seminary are only tools to be used to treasure carefully. Having said that, memory could also lead to despair if tied to dark moments of hatred and violence. Therefore memory is double edged but the power is unquestionable

Reminiscences

Memoirs of Serampore Trio are worth narrating. A desolating disaster occurred on 25th March 1812. It was the Serampore fire. "The immense printing-office, two hundred feet long and fifty broad, reduced to a mere shell. The yard covered with burnt quires of paper, the loss in article was immense. Carey walked over the smoking ruins. The tears stood in his eyes. 'In one short evening,' said he, 'the labours of years are consumed. How unsearchable are the ways of God! I had lately brought some things to the utmost perfection of which they seemed capable, and contemplated the missionary establishment with perhaps too much self-congratulation. The Lord has laid me low, that I may look more simply to Him.' (Life of William Carey: Shoemaker & Missionary by George Smith C.I.E., LL.D. 1909).

Carey had grossly underestimated what it would cost to come to India. Carey's early years were miserable and were forced to move his family repeatedly as he sought employment that could sustain them. Illness struck the family, and loneliness and regret set it: "I am in a strange land," he wrote, "no Christian friend, a large family, and nothing to supply their wants." But he also retained hope: "Well, I have God, and his word is sure." He learned Bengali with the help of a pundit, and in a few weeks began translating the Bible into Bengali and preaching to small gatherings. When Carey himself contracted malaria, and then his five year-old Peter died of dysentery, it became too much for his wife, Dorothy, whose mental reception deteriorated rapidly, suffered delusions, and threatening him with a knife. She eventually had to be confined to a room and physically restrained.

In October 1799, things finally turned when he was invited to locate in Serampore, a Danish settlement, near Calcutta. He then only came under the protection of the Danes, who permitted him to preach legally where as in the British-controlled areas of India, all of Carey's missionary work had been illegal. Carey was joined by William Ward, a printer, and Joshua and Hanna Marshman, teachers. Mission finances improved as Ward began securing government printing contracts, the Marshmans opened schools for children, and Carey began teaching at Fort William College in Calcutta. In December 1800, after seven years of missionary labor, Carey baptized his first convert, Krishna Pal, and two months later, he published his first Bengali New Testament. Carey and his pundits over the next twenty eight years translated the entire Bible into India's major languages: Bengali, Oriya, Marathi, Hindi, Assamese, and Sanskrit and parts of other languages and dialects. He also sought social reform in India, including the abolition of infanticide, widow burning (*sati*), and assisted suicide. By the time Carey died, he had spent forty years in India and his mission could count only some 700 converts in a nation of millions. According to our modern day church growth theory, his mission was a total failure but we are gathered here to celebrate that failure which had laid an impressive foundation of Bible translations, education, and social reform.

The relationship between the Home Committee with their supporters on the one hand and the Serampore group on the other were ideal until the arrival of John Dyer as the Society's secretary from 1817-54. His letters were described by Carey as 'commercial letters' and the missionaries felt themselves to be ranked simply as 'paid agents'. The story is unpleasant but very much part of the Serampore mission memoir. It was perhaps inevitable that the ageing group of missionaries with properties they had planned, built and paid for, the chain of mission stations and last but not the least a close-knit community with its very special financial basis of arrangements, should have presented a difficult set of problems to a committee far away in London. The question of property and trusteeship, matters of authority and control were elevated above grateful recognition of unparalleled services, sacrifices and the saintliness of the trio whose place in history will remain secure. (William Carey: J.B.Middlebrook, London,1961)

Multiple Voices

We are overwhelmed by the numerous voices of our time. It was not audible when Vikas Swaroop wrote the novel but it became not only audible but also loud when 'Slumdog Millionaire' started winning awards. "Slum is not other India. Dharavi is not an aberration. It is both a condemnation and celebration of what we are, we need to own it, change it, admire it and hate it" (Santosh Desai Times of India, 26.1.09}. The voices of victims of violence in Kondhmal of Orissa in 2008, series of bomb blasts, 26/11 Mumbai terror and the cry of the vulnerable, disinherited, discriminated, stigmatized, battered and abused are shocking. The voice of the market is worlds apart. "35=10, the instructor wrote in big bold letters on the black board. Remember the instructor said to the class, a thirty five year old American's brain and IQ is the same as a ten-year old Indian's brain. This will help you to understand your clients. You need to be as patient as you are when dealing with a child (Chetan Bhagat, One night @ the Call center). The novel is a caricature of our society where a dynamic young, skilled, articulate professionals work though the night functioning under a different time, pretending to be familiar with a climate and culture they have never experienced, enjoying a life style: a cocktail of premature affluence and westernization transplanted to an Indian setting.

It was thunderstorm when Lehman Brothers went under in September 2008 that continues to drench all but particularly caught the young who were used to hop from one job to another, from one swollen pay cheque to another, from one globe-trotting assignment to the other. When greed and power overtook then it was not difficult for the pathfinder of Satyam to inflate income, profits and cash reserves. The fraud reveals the appalling system failure and pathetic state of corporate governance. Three decades ago, CEOs typically earned 30 to 40 times the income of ordinary workers. Last year, CEOs of large public companies averaged 344 times the average pay of workers. John Kenneth Galbraith, the great economist, once explained: "The salary of the chief executive of a large corporation is not a market award for achievement. It is frequently in the nature of a warm personal gesture by the individual to himself."(The Week, January 25, 2009) Seminaries also seem to be overwhelmed with the voices of the arithmetic of number of students, generating funds to meet the cost of management and struggling to retain faculty members than retaining affordable fee structure for the marginalized, hearing the voice of the overwhelming majority of our people in villages and improving the quality of service. It is not isolated sight in some seminaries where the students have to accommodate in bunk-beds as if reading theology in Railway compartment. Perhaps we seem to have lost the spirit as self preservation has become our preoccupation.

A Yearning

There is a phenomenal yearning for a spirituality being manifested through our local congregations challenging the formality, structure and prerogatives of our historical churches. These outbursts are not sporadic and can not be ignored. People are searching for answers to complex questions of a rapidly changing world. Spiritual formation is an integral part of theological education. The core issue lies in realization of the presence of God. The word in Bible to denote God's presence (panim) is at the same time the ordinary word for human face. The relation between these two meanings could be found in the story of Jacob's encounter with God at Penuel. By necessity Jacob is forced to return to the territory of the brother he had cheated of his inheritance. When he hears that Esau is coming to meet with four hundred men, his guilty conscience suggests the worst, devised a scheme for survival at least some of his family and possessions. In the extremity of his distress on the occasion Jacob wrestles in prayer and sees God 'face to face' (Gen 32:30). The next morning as Esau runs to meet his brother and falls weeping on his neck, Jacob cries "For to see your face is like seeing the face of God, now that you have received me favorably" (Gen 33:10). To focus on this encounter is not to reduce the divinity of God but to sensitize the presence that requires of wrestling and listening in silence the voice of God. Dietrich Bonhoeffer had called for a period of public silence by the church in 1940s. It demanded a self-discipline which would give time to listen penitently to others and in which it would wait for God to renew the language of proclamation. Truth is an integral part of listening and rooted in innocence but not in ignorance.

A Commentary

The history of Protestant missions is in many ways an extended commentary on the phrase 'Expect great things from God and Attempt great things for God' based on the text:" Enlarge the place of your tent, stretch your tent curtains wide, do not hold back; lengthen your cords, strengthen your stakes" (Isaiah 54:2). It is not a question of how fast we can go, how fast we can grow in number and how fast we can work. Sometimes it appears as if we are like the person on a horse galloping swiftly along the road. He was asked by an old farmer standing in the field: where are you going? The rider turned around and shouted back, do not ask me, just ask my horse? Doing truth means to follow the footprints of Jesus of Nazareth with non-negotiable values. January 20th 2009 was historic when a black person stepped into white house. It symbolizes a genuine revolution in a country where blacks were bought and sold as slaves and kept apart and where some forty years before a Baptist minister and civil right leader Martin Luther King Jr. in his famous speech had said "I have a dream that my four little children will one day live in a nation where they will not be judged by the color of their skins but by the content of their character". A successor of that dream, President Barack Hussein Obama in his inaugural Address said "Our challenges may be new. The instruments with which we meet them may be new. But those values upon which our success depends—honesty and hard work, courage and fair play, tolerance and curiosity, loyalty and patriotism—these things are old. These things are true. They have been the quiet force of progress throughout our history". Basic values are timeless like the legacy of trio of Serampore. It shall continue to shape the minds of thousands that pass through our esteemed institutions of learning.

A Commitment

'Oikoumene' needs to be a space for meaningful engagements. A commitment of 'doing truth' would require taking risk. Some advise not to take risk. "Not to take a risk when it is time to take a risk is the biggest risk of all" What prevents us from taking a decision is the fear of change. Fear of change is loss of control and loss of power that results in resistance to change. Insights of wider commitment beyond boundaries in the mission of God are not only inspiring but also educative. Can anything good come out of Chandpur Bela locality of Patna? Once Patna math wizard Anand used to hawk "papad" to earn a living. His father used to work in the postal department until his premature death and his mother used to prepare papad. His noble initiative of Super30 in partnership with Abhayanand is to coach thirty economically weak students for IIT-JEE free of cost for seven months away from home with home-cook food prepared by Anand's mother Jayanti Devi. The result was 18 in 2003, 22 in 2004, 26 in 2005, 28 in 2006 and 30 in 2007.

It will be a decisive commitment if five main families of the Christian community: Roman Catholic, Orthodox, historic Protestant, Evangelical and Pentecostal can be brought into an 'intentional fellowship' in common engagement for witness and service. One experiment is 'Global Christian Forum' The idea of a Forum goes back to the suggestion made by Rev Dr Konrad Raiser in the mid-1990, then General Secretary of the World Council of Churches on the recognition that neither the Roman Catholic Church nor the overwhelming majority of Evangelical and Pentecostal churches were part of WCC and that a broader and more inclusive pattern of relationship was called for. Global Christian Forum event in 2007 in Nairobi was a culmination of consultations in four major regions of the world: Asia, Africa, Europe and Latin America from 2004-6. It also reflects local initiative taken independently in the formation of National United Christian Forum consisting of National Council of Churches in India, Evangelical fellowship of India and Catholic Bishops Conference of India. The Global as well as National Forum is a space for encounter, a space where trust can grow and new relationship can be established. It may sound naïve but a crucial element in all forum meetings have been the simple exercise of sharing personal faith journeys by the individual participants. It has proven to be a powerful means not only of discovering the faith convictions that are held in common by Christians coming from different traditions but also building trust and friendship.

My best wishes and prayers for my dear students is that you may be able to act justly and to love mercy and to walk humbly with your God.

> "If you want to walk fast, walk alone;
> If you want go long way, walk together"

NB: Commemoration service address on 7th February 2007 on the Convocation Day of Serampore College (University) at Tamilnadu Theological Seminary, Madurai by Bishop D.K.Sahu, General Secretary, NCCI.

Appendices

I. Profile of a Journey

Dhirendra Kumar Sahu was born on 13th October, 1950, was baptized as a believer on 14th April 1968, ordained on 13th April, 1975, married to Manjusree Sahu on 15th April 1975 and was consecrated as bishop of the North India in the Diocese of Eastern Himalaya on 6th August, 2000. He started his schooling in Khurda, continued under graduate studies leading to Bachelor of Arts with economics honors from P. N. College, Khurda under Utkal University, Orissa. His first degree in theology was Bachelor of Divinity from Serampore College, then Master of Arts in Theology from the University of Oxford and later Doctor in Theology from the University of Birmingham, United Kingdom.

Theology Department of Serampore College : Period of service 1982-2000

- Lecturer in Christian Theology
- Assistant Professor of Christian Theology
- Professor of Christian Theology
- Dean: Theology Department, Serampore College
- Registrar: North India Institute of Post Graduate Theological Studies
- Vice-Principal: Theology Department, Serampore College

Visiting Faculty
- Aizwal Theological College, Mizoram
- Orthodox Theological Seminary, Nagpur

Pastoral Experience
Ordained Presbyter of the Church of North India

- The Diocese of Cuttack
- The Diocese of Calcutta
- The Diocese of Barrackpore

Diocesan Bishop of the Church of North India in the Diocese of Eastern Himalaya

Ecumenical Responsibility
General Secretary, National Council of Churches in India

Elected Responsibilities
- Member of the Senate of Serampore College (1982-88)
- Editor: Indian Journal of Theology (1992-2000)
- Member of the Senate of Serampore College (1993-2000)
- Chairperson: Theological Commission of Church of North India (2001-2004)
- Chairperson: Commission on Mission of Church of North India (2001-2004)
- Member of Synodical Board of Social Services of Church of North India (2001-2004)
- Member of the Coordination Committee of Senate of Serampore (2002-2005)
- Member of the Honorary D.D. Committee of Senate of Serampore (2002-2003)
- Member: Continuation Committee of United and Uniting Churches, WCC (2002-8)

- Member of Honorary D.D. Committee of Senate of Serampore(University) 2008-9

- Editor, NCC Review (2005-2009)

- Joint Secretary of National United Christian Forum of NCCI-CBCI-EFI (2005-2009)

- Member of the Senate of Serampore College 2002-

- Member of the Executive Committee of the Christian Medical College, Vellore (2007-11)

- Co-opted member of the Christian Medical College Council (2010-11)

- Member of the Trans World Radio-India 2010-

Books

- United & Uniting: A Story of the Church of North India. ISPCK, 2001, pp xvi+ 121.

- The Church of North India: A Historical and Systematic Theological Inquiry into an Ecumenical Ecclesiology. Peter Lang: Frankfurt am Main, 1994, pp xi + 354.

Published Articles and Public Lectures

1. 'From Hostility to Hospitality' (in press) BTESSC, Paper presented in D.Th Coloquium on 'People with Disability' held at Bangalore from 12-14th November, 2009, Bangalore.

2. Perspectives and Issues in Mission and Interfaith Relations: Christian participation in Nation Building: Pre-Edinburgh Consultation (in press) held at UTC, Bangalore,17-19 July, 2009.

3. Human Sexuality: A Legal Perspective, Religion and Society, Dec.2009, pp. 37-44.

4. Eucharist and Ecumenical Movement in India, In: Eucharist and Community- Beyond All Barriers: A Theological Forum in preparation for FABC 2009, pp. 77-89.

5. Telling the Truth and Living the Truth: *Commemoration Service Address,* Serampore College Convocation, 2009, pp. 1-8.

6. *What* does the Lord require of us?" In: Lenten Lantern, 2009, NCCI, p. 1.

7. Repositioning Dalits & Tribals in Local Congregations: Mission Challenges, NCC Review, August, 2008, p. 332.

8. *A Gathered Community of Witness & Service;*In:Global Christian Forum: Transforming Ecumenism, ed: Richard Howell, EFI, 2007, pp. 130-139.

9. *Towards an Understanding of Justice & Peace in Mission with the Marginalized,* Ed. Samuel W Meshak, Christava Sahitya Samiti, Tiruvalla, March, 2007, pp. 533-40.

10. *Mission and Ministry: Challenges from the Ecumenical Movement,* ISPCK, 2007. Bishop and Mrs Parmar Lecture series, LTC Jabalpur, 22-24 November, 2006.

11. *Congregational Empowerment for Dalit Liberation,* NCC Review, April, 2007, p. 62.

12. *Educating the Educated,* NCC Review, Jan-Feb, 2007, p. 21.

13. *Mapping the Oikoumene in India,* NCC Review, March,2006, p. 22-34.

14. *Role of Church in Nation Building,* NCC Review, Nov. 2005, p. 494.

15. *Beyond Dialogue,* NCC Review, September, 2005, p. 370.

16. *Mission and Ecumenism: An Opportunity & Challenge,* In: Shepherd of a Pilgrim People, Ed. G. Sobhanam & V.Victor, ISPCK, 2005, pp. 40-46.

17. Towards a Transformed & Transforming Community, ed. Enos Das Pradhan & Sudipta Singh, CNI-ISPCK, 2005, pp. 38-44.

18. Toward a Transforming Church of North India: Church on the Move, ISPCK, 2005.

19. *The Church of North India:* In: Encyclopaedia of Christianity in India, Jnana-Deepa Vidyapeeth, 2005.

20. *Ministry from the Margin*, Indian Journal of Theology, 2005.

21. *Christian Participation in Nation Building*, CSI Life, 2005.

22. *Micro Ecumenism, India*: God of All Grace, Ed. Joseph George, ATC & UTC, 2005, pp. 403-10.

23. *Management: A Possibility for Transformation*, In:Christian Manager, Dec-Jan, 2005.

24. *Spirituality of Reconciliation: Theological Justification for Active Non-violence*, pp. 53-66 In: Towards a Culture of Peace in South Asia, Ed:S.Prabhakar,BTESSC/SATHRI, 2004.

25. *A Case Study on Identity: The Communion of Churches in India*, p105-14, In: With a Demonstration of the Spirit and of Power, Faith and Order Paper No 195, WCC, 2004.

26. *Individuals, Institutions and Imagination In: Together With People* Ed: Samson Prabhakar, SATHRI/BTESSC, 2004.

27. *Recognizing the Structure: A Possibility for Mission Today*, In: Church's Participation in Theological Education, Ed. S.Prabhakar & M. J. Joseph, BTESSC, 2003, pp. 12-19.

28. *Visionary Household of God*, Bishop Thomas Mar Athanasius Memorial Lecture. Kottayam, Kerala, India, 21-23rd November, 2003.

29. *Evangelical-Ecumenical: From Polarity to Convergence*. NCC Review, Jan-Feb, 2003.

30. *A Search for an Inter-Cultural Ecclesial Identity, Inter-Cultural Asian Theological Methodologies: An Exploration* Ed: Samson Prabhakar,South Asia Theological Research Institute, Bangalore, 2002.

31. *Episcopacy in Church of North India*, North India Church Review: May, 2001, p. 3.

32. *Pedagogy of Transformative Process*, In Ripples: A Journey of CNI SBSS, ISPCK, 2001.

33. *Building on What Unites: Overcoming What Divides*, NCC Review, February-March, 2000.

34. Mission and Transformation: Canon Subir Biswas Memorial Silver Jubilee Celebration Lecture 1999, St. Paul's Cathedral & Cathedral Relief Service, Calcutta.

35. *Theological Education in India: A Profile*, In: Building Communities for Celebration and Resistance, Compiled by V.S.Lall, September, 1998.

36. *Partners in Creation: A Forgotten Paradigm*, Gurukul Summer Institute, April, 1998.

37. *Spirit of Ecumenism: Retrospect & Prospect*, North India Church Review, July, 1996.

38. *Christian Faith and Economic Justice* 20th Bishop Joshi Memorial Lecture.A Build Publication: November, 1996.

39. *A Response to the Paper: Salvation from an African Perspective.* Mugabe, H. J. Indian Journal of Theology, Vol. 36/No. 1/ 1994.

40. *Serampore Then & Now.* Indian Journal of Theology, Vol. 35/ No 1/ 1993.

Participation in International Consultations-Forums

1. Christian Conference of Asia General Assembly, 14-21 April, 2010, Malayasia.

2. Consultation: Mekong Ecumenical Partnership, Chiangmai, 30-3 August, 2009.

3. Consultation on Eucharist and Community- Beyond All Barriers: A Theological Forum of Asian Roman Catholic Church in preparation for Federation of Asian Bishops Conference in 2009, 17-21 May, 2009, Seol. Korea.

4. Peace, Security and Development in South Asia, 30th -2nd April 2009, Bangalore.

5. Global Ecumenical Conference on Dalit Liberation, 20-24th March 2009, Bangkok.

6. Sixth Congress of Asian theologians, Iloilo, 9-13th February 2009, Philippines.

7. Christian Conference of Asia: Theological Workshop, 12-16 Nov, 2008, Bangkok.

8. Global Christian Forum, 8-11th November, 2008, New Delhi.

9. Eighth Consultation of United & Uniting Churches,29-5th Nov 2008, Johannesburg.

10. Asia General Secretaries Meeting, 31st-3rd September 2008, Bangladesh.

11. Consultation on Tradition & Modernity, 26-28 July 2008, Bangkok.

12. Dialogue on Mission for South Asia, 29-2nd April, 2008, UTC, Bangalore.

13. Global Christian Forum, 6-12 November, 2007, Kenya.

14. Consultation Role of Church for Peace and Unification in Korean Peninsula, 8-13 August, 2007, Seoul, Korea.

15. Asian Movement for Christian Unity(AMCU-IV),11- 14 June 2007, Kuala Lumpur, Malayasia.

16. United and Uniting Churches Meeting,26th February - 1st March, 2007, Geneva.

17. Global Christian Forum in Asia, CCA-FABC & EFI, 19-24 September, 2006, Bangkok.

18. WCC Central Committee Meeting, 29th August 7th September,2006, Geneva. Consultation on Revitalizing Ecumenical Movement in Asia Today, 6-11th May 2006, Phnom Penh, Cambodia.

19. 9th *WCC General Assembly 13-26th February*, 2006, Porto Alegre, Brazil.

20. Consultation on Proposed Ecumenical Alliance for Development, December 2005, Bossey, Geneva.

21. South Asia Regional Capacity Building Training: Bangladesh August, 2005, & Kathmandu, Nepal November 2005.

22. Ecumenical Enablers' Training Programme: February 2005, Bangkok, Thailand.

23. Ecumenical Leadership Development, Colombo, 1-5 July 2005.

24. Consultation on Development Goals in Asia: Our Diaconal responses,29-30th June 2005, Colombo, Srilanka.

25. Asia-Africa Forum: Spirit of Bandung:Towards a Common Forum,12-14th April, 2005, Jakarta, Indonesia.

26. CCA General Assembly, 31st March-5th April, 2005, Chiang Mai, Thailand.

27. Second Anglican Contextual Theologian Consultation, 2-6 August 2004, Durban, South Africa.

28. Anglican Contextual Theologians Consultation, May 2003, Cambridge, MA, USA.

29. Dialogues between World Alliance of Reformed Churches and Disciples, March 2003, Cambridge, United Kingdom.

30. Seventh Consultation of United and Uniting Churches, Sept., 2002, Netherlands.

31. International Consultation on Intercultural Methodologies, April 2002, Sri Lanka.

32. Dialogues between World Alliance of Reformed Churches and Disciples, January 2002, Geneva, Switzerland.

33. Dialogue between World Alliance of Baptist Churches and Anglican Communion.

34. Baptist International Conference on Theological Education, 1993, South Africa.

Participation in National Consultations-Forums

1. D.Th Colloquium on 'People with Disability': BTESSC,12-14th November, 2009, Bangalore.

2. Pre-centenary Edinburgh Consultation 2010, UTC Bangalore17-19, July 2009.

3. National Convention of Christian Endeavour in India: 15-17 May, 2009, Bangalore.

4. Conference of Principals of Christian Colleges in India, 4-6th

May 2009, Ecumenical Christian Center, Whitefield, Bangalore.

5. Pre-Election 15th Lokshava Consultation: Divisive Politics to Inclusive Democracy 1-3rd April, 2009, New Delhi.

6. Consultation on Anglican Urban Network: India chapter, 19-22nd June, 2008.

7. National Consultation on HIV & AIDS, ECC Bangalore 26-28th March, 2008.

8. World Fellowship of Inter-religious Councils, 4-7 October, 2008, Cochin.

9. National Conference of Nurses League, CMAI, Nov 7-9, Secunderabad, 2006.

10. National Consultation on Curriculum Revision in Theological Education 24-25th October 2006, YMCA, Chennai.

11. National Consultation on Rerouting Asia Mission and Ecumenism,19-22nd May 2006, Chennai, CCA-URM

12. All India Council of Christian Women, 27th October, 2005, YMCA, New Delhi

13. Institute of Revisioning of Mission: Address on Denominationalism vis-à-vis Ecumenism HPDCenter, Nagpur, India, 12-02-2003.

14. A Consultation on Men & Women in God's Mission: Delivered Keynote Address, Bishop Heber College, Tiruchirapalli, India, 14-16th November 2001.

15. Theological Education in North India: A Consultation on Priority of Theological Education, BTE SSC, CNI Bhavan, New Delhi 23-24th April, 2001.

16. Millenium Youth Festival Church of North India, Ranchi, 16-18 January, 2000.

17. Church in Dialogue: Keynote Address in the 37th North India Theological Students Conference.

18. Consultation on Congregation in Mission, CNISBSS, Shimla, 24-28 June, 1998.

19. All India Pastors' Conference: Address on Ecumenism, Kalimpong, West Bengal, 28-31st July, 1996.

20. Rural Laity: A Ministry of Empowerment: Board of Theological Education of Senate of Serampore College, Cuttack, Orissa, 21-25th May, 1996.

21. CNI Consultation on Financial Management, Dhyan Ashram, Calcutta, 18-20 March, 1996.

22. Equipping Church for an Alternative Vision,ESII, Durgapur,18-20 September, 1995.

23. Consultation on Christian Stewardsip, CNI Bhavan, New Delhi, 2-4 March, 1995.

24. The Emerging Socio-Economic and Political Order in India: A Theological Response: Keynote Address, North India Theological Students Conference, 1993.

Contributors

Rev. Dr. David F. Ford is currently Regius Professor of Divinity at the University of Cambridge. Earlier he taught at University of Birmingham. He studied Classics at Trinity College Dublin, and later Theology in Cambridge, Yale, and Tübingen. He is the author of numerous books, including *Christian Wisdom. Desiring God and Learning in Love* (Cambridge, 2007), *The Shape of Living* (London, 2002), *Theology: A Very Short Introduction* (Oxford, 2000) and *Self and Salvation: Being Transformed* (Cambridge, 1999), and is a member of the editorial board of a number of major journals. He is the Director of the Cambridge Inter-Faith Programme.

Dr. Nicholas J. Wood, Dean, Director of the Centre for Christianity and Culture; Director of the MTh; Tutorial Fellow in Religion and Culture at Regents Park College. Within the University of Oxford he has been a member of the Faculty of Theology since 1995 and has played a major role in the implementation and development of the M.Th in Applied Theology Degree. He delivered the Whitley Lectures (Manchester, Oxford, London and Cardiff) for 2002 and the McCandless Lecture at Georgetown College, Kentucky. He is a Baptist Minister.

The Rev. Dr. Richard Howell, General Secretary of the Evangelical Fellowship of India, General Secretary, Asia Evangelical Alliance. He was the Principal of Allahabad Bible Seminary where he was the Professor of Theology. He is deeply involved in the affairs of

Christians in India, especially issues related to atrocities, privileges of minorities under constitutions and wider ecumenism.

Rev. Dr. M. Mani Chacko, Ph.D (Lond.) is the Director, Ecumenical Christian Centre, Bangalore. He is also the Presbyter of the CSI Central Kerala Diocese. Formerly he was the principal of the Gurukul Lutheran Theological College and Research Institute, Chennai. He was the Professor of Old Testament at Gurukul and Serampore College, and has written books and articles in the area of specializations.

Dr. Kalarikkal Poulose Aleaz is Professor of Religions at Bishop's College as well as Professor and Dean of Doctoral Programme of North India Institute of Post-Graduate Theological Studies, Kolkata. He was William Patron Fellow of the Sally Oaks Colleges, Birmingham and visiting Professor at Harford Seminary, USA as well as at University of South Africa, Pretoria. He also delivered Teape Lectures in Universities of Cambridge, Birmingham and Edinburgh in 2005. He is a prolific writer and has written many books and articles.

Rev. Dr. Wati Longchar is Dean of Doctor of Ministry and Extension Programme of the Senate Centre For Extension and Pastoral Theological Research (SCEPTRE), a wing of the Senate of Serampore College (University) as well as the Director-in-charge of South Asia Theological Research Institute of the Board of Theological Education of the Senate of Serampore College (BTESSC), Bangalore. He earlier served in the ETE-WCC and was Professor of Theology at Eastern Theological College, Jorhat, Assam. He is an acknowledged scholar of Tribal/indigenous Theology and has authored many books.

Dr. Siga Arles, is currently the Director of the Indian Institute of Missiology. The **Indian Institute of Missiology–Research Centre**, Bangalore, offers the Ph.D. programme in Missiology so as to develop faculty members for mission training institutes, theological colleges, and biblical seminaries across India. **Siga Arles** was Dean of the

Consortium for Indian Missiological Education, Bangalore, and formerly Vice-principal and Professor of Missiology at Serampore College. The doctoral program was developed in partnership with the **India Missions Association**. He also edits the ATA's Journal of Asian Evangelical Theology and IIM's Journal of Indian Missiology.

Rev. Dr. Pratap Chandra Gine is Vice-Principal of Serampore College (Theology Department). He is also Professor of New Testament in the same college, Registrar, North India institute of Post-Graduate Theological Studies (NIIPGTS), and the Coordinator, Diploma in Bible Translation, Theology Department, Serampore College. He served as Deputy Registrar of the Senate and also taught at Eastern Theological College, Jorhat.

Mr. Ashis Sahu, completed his undergraduate studies in finance and economics with a summa-cum-laude distinction from the university of Kansas, USA and his post graduate studies in financial management from the University of Durham, U.K. He works as a consultant with Capgemini in London, focusing on how businesses can make their financial operations more efficient. He has a strong interest in development initiatives in India. He is youngest son of Bishop Sahu.

Mr. Sanjay Patra, F.C.A., M. Com., MDP, at present is Executive Director, Financial Management Service Foundation. He is a Chartered Accountant by profession. He has been deeply involved in the development sector in India since 20 years. Since 1999, he is with Financial Management Service Foundation (FMSF) which is a unit set up by Evangelischer Entwicklungsdientst or EED. He has written a number of books on the area of his work and specialization.

Rev. Surendra Kumar Sahu, is the Senior Manager for the Bible Society of India, Bangalore. He is an active Member of the Pastoral Team at St. Mark's Cathedral, Bangalore. He is a member of the Executive Committee in the World Christian Endeavor Union. He joined as an auditor and was promoted to a senior Accounts Manager in the Auditor-General office, Bhubaneswar. He was the Orissa Auxillary Secretary of Bible Society of India. He has completed his M.A. in Public Admistration and L.L.B from Utkal University. He followed that up with a Masters in Theology from Westminster College, Oxford, UK.

EDITORS

Mr. Bibhudutta Sahu is post-graduate in Political Science, and is working with Church of North Indian Synod as the Program Facilitator, Synodical Board of Social Services, Resource Center for Social Action – Orissa. He is a LEAD (Leadership for Environment and Development) India Fellow. He is currently based in Bhubaneswar. He has been working with the grassroots communities in West Bengal and Maharashtra for 10 years. He is the eldest son of Bishop Sahu.

Prof Dr. Ravi Tiwari, since 2004, is Registrar, Senate of Serampore College (University). He was the Principal of John Robert's Theological Seminary, Shillong (1995-97), Vice-Principal, Department of Theology, Serampore College (1987-92) and Dean of Doctoral and Post-graduate studies at Gurukul Lutheran Theological College and Research Institute, Chennai (1999-2005). He taught Philosophy and Religions at various theological colleges since 1979. He is the author of two notable books, Yesudas: Witness of a Convert (2000) and Reflections and Studies in Religion (2008) and written many articles in the fields of religion and theological education.